BATTLE

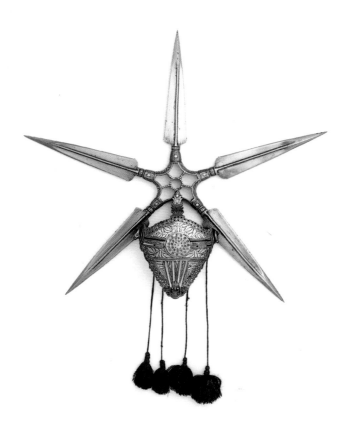

Dutch wheel-
lock pistol

Indian
spiked mace

British
shoulder scales

French
footsoldier's
backpack

British
shoulder
belt plate

Italian
linstock

Polish or
Hungarian
war hammer

U.S. Gatling gun

EYEWITNESS BOOKS

BATTLE

Turkish Order
of Osmanieh

British
Victoria Cross

Written by
DR. RICHARD HOLMES

Photographed by
GEOFF DANN & GEOFF BRIGHTLING

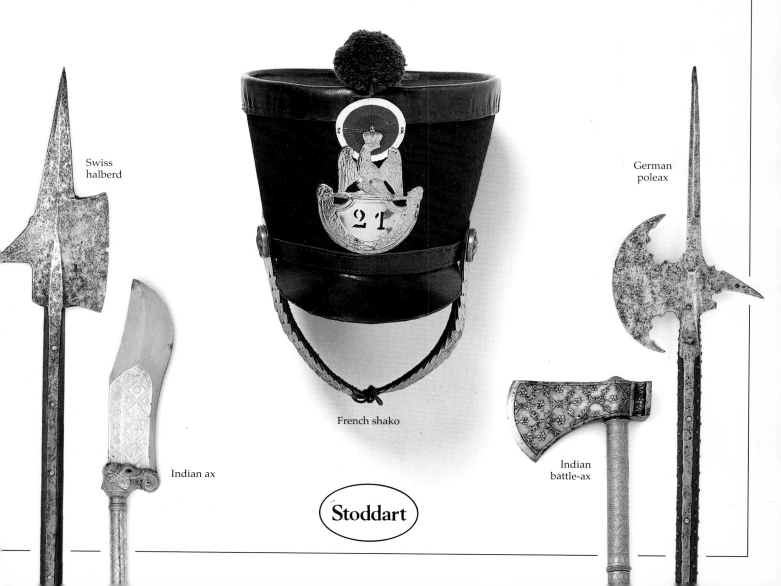

Swiss
halberd

German
poleax

French shako

Indian ax

Indian
battle-ax

Stoddart

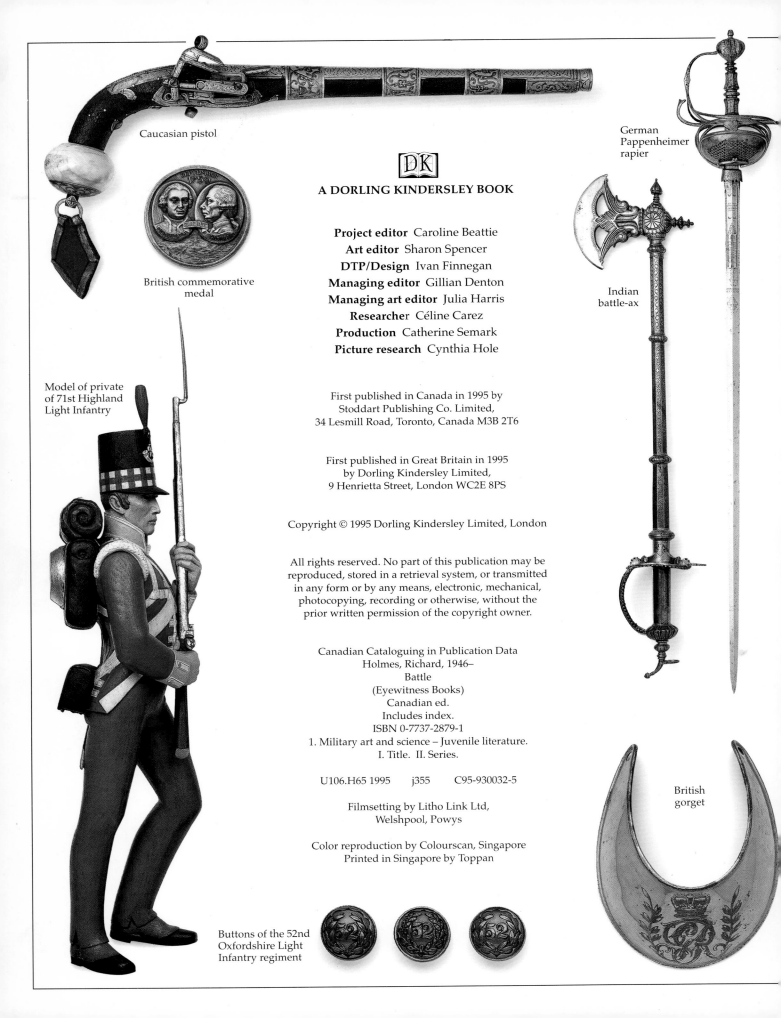

Caucasian pistol

British commemorative medal

German Pappenheimer rapier

Indian battle-ax

Model of private of 71st Highland Light Infantry

DK

A DORLING KINDERSLEY BOOK

Project editor Caroline Beattie
Art editor Sharon Spencer
DTP/Design Ivan Finnegan
Managing editor Gillian Denton
Managing art editor Julia Harris
Researcher Céline Carez
Production Catherine Semark
Picture research Cynthia Hole

First published in Canada in 1995 by
Stoddart Publishing Co. Limited,
34 Lesmill Road, Toronto, Canada M3B 2T6

First published in Great Britain in 1995
by Dorling Kindersley Limited,
9 Henrietta Street, London WC2E 8PS

Canadian Cataloguing in Publication Data
Holmes, Richard, 1946–
Battle
(Eyewitness Books)
Canadian ed.
Includes index.
ISBN 0-7737-2879-1
1. Military art and science – Juvenile literature.
I. Title. II. Series.

U106.H65 1995   j355   C95-930032-5

Filmsetting by Litho Link Ltd,
Welshpool, Powys

Color reproduction by Colourscan, Singapore
Printed in Singapore by Toppan

British gorget

Buttons of the 52nd Oxfordshire Light Infantry regiment

Contents

Japanese Order
of the Rising Sun

What is battle?

BATTLE IS A CLASH between groups of armed people. It occurs in most cultures and on all continents. Its character – the duration, the number of participants, the weapons, and the tactics employed – is infinitely variable. Battle is intimately bound up with the social, economic, technical, and political features of its age. In the European tradition it was a way for the rulers of one country to force those of another to comply with their wishes. Asian cultures often avoided battle and sought to win by rapid movement or protracted operations. Battle presented many challenges to the courage and resolve of combatants. The German military theorist Carl von Clausewitz (1780–1831) warned that "the character of battle ... is slaughter, and its price is blood."

Original statue would have had spear fitted into right hand

CYPRIOT WARRIORS
These terra-cotta figurines, made in Cyprus in the 7th century B.C., remind us that a battle is a collective enterprise. The warriors, dressed in armor combining metal plates with fabric, would have held spears and fought in close formation.

Spear

The hoplon gave Greek soldiers the name hoplite

Greave being fitted

Bronze helmet

WARRIORS DRESSING
The male members of the city-states of ancient Greece had to serve as soldiers when their city went to war. They did military service and kept fit in case they were called up. Greek warriors were armed with a bronze helmet and shinguards called greaves. Each carried a *hoplon*, a heavy shield, on their left arm. They fought in a mass called a phalanx, closely packed together so that the hoplon protected the right side of the man to the left. A long spear was their main weapon.

FLEEING ARABS
The great battles of history were often short – the effort of plying a sword or a spear quickly exhausted combatants. Defeated warriors fled, and might escape by throwing away their heavy weapons and equipment. Training and discipline were battle winners. The Assyrians, who lived in the area of modern Iraq in c. 1300–600 B.C., were fierce and well organized; these Arabs are fleeing from them.

CHARGING THE ENEMY
The Egyptians enjoyed a long period of military ascendancy. This wall painting shows Pharaoh Sethos I (ruled 1318–1304 B.C.) charging the Libyans in his chariot. War chariots were generally used only by the privileged members of the army.

Helmet would have been topped by a crest

WARRIOR ON HORSEBACK
This bronze statue of a warrior on his horse was made at Taranto in southern Italy in about 550 B.C. The horse was of immense military importance. It helped warriors cover ground quickly on campaign, and in battle horsemen could ride down unprotected footsoldiers.

Hands would have held shield and spear

A CLASH OF TWO SIDES
Armored knights (the French on the left and the English on the right) at the battle of Poitiers in France in 1356. The physical and psychological demands of combat led to the development of warrior classes, like the European knight and the Japanese samurai, whose very existence was geared to fighting battles.

Horse and warrior were cast separately

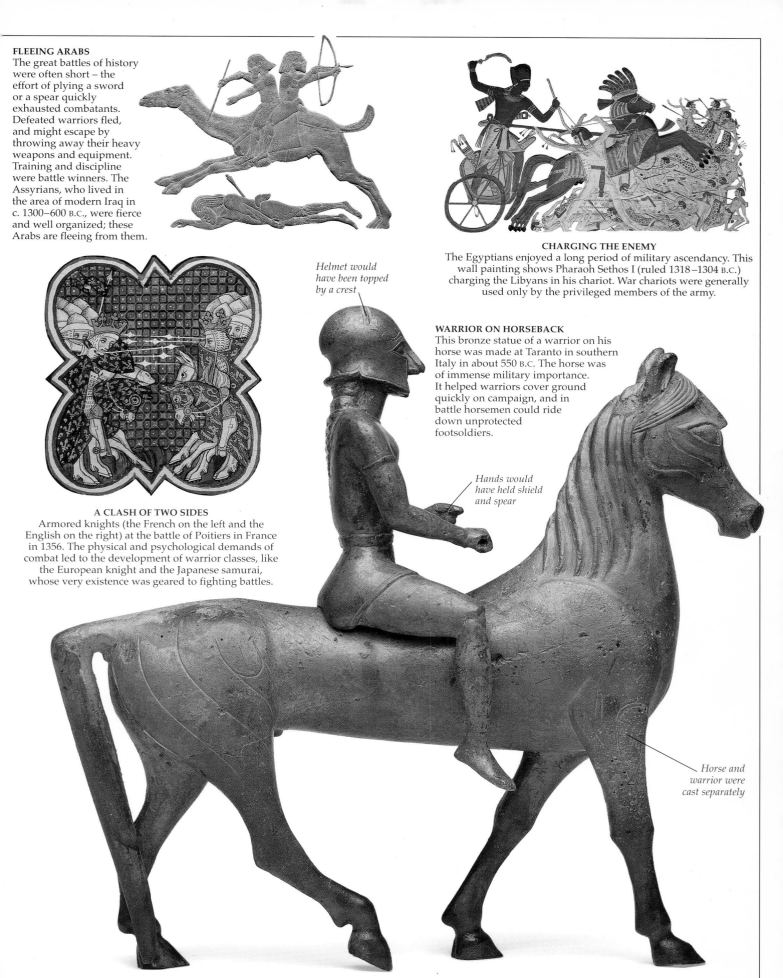

Infantry of the line

INFANTRY FORMED THE GREAT MASS of most armies, and unskilled recruits who volunteered for or were conscripted (drafted) into service would usually serve as footsoldiers. In the 18th and 19th centuries, infantry units formed an army's line of battle, so they were called regiments of the line. Regiments were numbered or named after a geographical region; sometimes they were known by the names of their colonels. There were specialist infantry, such as light regiments or rifle regiments, intended for skirmishing, and grenadiers, initially formed to use a hand grenade, but later simply elite footsoldiers.

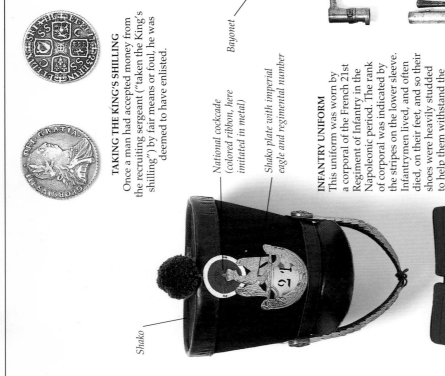

JOIN UP! JOIN UP!
Although the Pressing Act of 1704 meant that jobless able-bodied men could be forced into military service, the British army usually relied on volunteers. A drummer would "beat up" to attract them, and a recruiting sergeant or officer would use cash and promises of regular meals and pay to persuade them to enlist.

"I WANT YOU FOR THE U.S. ARMY"
Posters appealed to the patriotic spirit, so as to avoid conscription (forced military service).

Bayonet

TAKING THE KING'S SHILLING
Once a man had accepted money from the recruiting sergeant ("taken the King's shilling") by fair means or foul, he was deemed to have enlisted.

National cockade (colored ribbon, here imitated in metal)

Shako plate with imperial eagle and regimental number

INFANTRY UNIFORM
This uniform was worn by a corporal of the French 21st Regiment of Infantry in the Napoleonic period. The rank of corporal was indicated by the stripes on the lower sleeve. Infantrymen lived, and often died, on their feet, and so their shoes were heavily studded to help them withstand the rigors of campaigning.

Chevron on upper sleeve awarded for five years' good conduct

Shako

Owner's initials

REPAIR KIT
The hussif (derived from the word *housewife*) was a case for needles, thread, and other bits of sewing equipment. This example was made from pieces of old uniform, embroidered with the owner's regimental colors (pp. 18–19), those of the Scottish 93rd Highlanders. It could be rolled up and put in the pack during travel or hung by the soldier's bedside in camp.

Corporal's stripes

AMMUNITION POUCH
This pouch was worn over the left shoulder on its buff leather strap, which incorporated a fitting for the bayonet. It also had a soft cap fastened beneath it.

This 1777-pattern Charleville musket (pp. 42–43) was the most common weapon of the French infantry

SHORT SWORD
The short sword was carried by most Napoleonic French infantrymen. Its value in combat was limited, but it was put to many illicit uses, such as chopping wood or holding a kettle over the campfire in bivouacs (open-air camps).

Studs helped shoes to last longer

DRESSED FOR THE WEATHER
Infantrymen carried warm, long greatcoats, which they wore in wet or cold weather. These members of the British 1st Foot Guards are in full marching order (equipment), with packs and cooking utensils on their backs.

FOOTSOLDIERS
Infantrymen fought on foot. Their uniforms served to clothe and protect them from the weather as well as to give each side a distinctive look – the British are in red and the French are in blue.

Brass buckle

Loose-fitting trousers were worn for battle over close-fitting knee breeches

PACK
The Napoleonic infantryman's pack was made from the hide of almost any animal that came to hand, and often had the fur left on to make it more hardwearing. It contained spare clothing and personal effects, and items like a greatcoat or spare shoes could be strapped to the outside.

Brass buttons embossed with "21," the regimental number

Heavy cavalry

FOR MUCH OF HISTORY, cavalry formed two main groups: the light cavalry's chief tasks were screening (counter-reconnaissance), scouting, and the pursuit of a beaten enemy; heavy cavalry were used for shock action (the physical impact of horses and people) on the field of battle. Heavy cavalry, whose function can be traced back to knights, were trained for the knee-to-knee charge, in which cavalry charged in solid lines. Heavy cavalry were used against both cavalry and infantry. Although it was difficult for even the best cavalry to ride down infantry who stood steady against the onslaught, the thunderous onrush of big men on big horses was very effective, and it often persuaded shaky infantry to run. Cuirassiers were the classic type of heavy cavalry, whose prestige helped ensure their survival into the early 20th century. A third category of cavalry, dragoons, began as footsoldiers on horseback; they did most of their fighting on foot, but were eventually regarded as true cavalry.

CHARGE!
French cuirassiers charge the Germans in the Franco-Prussian War of 1870–71. The cuirass alone could weigh as much as 12–15 lb (5.5–6.8 kg).

Snaffle bit

Curb bit

BIT BETWEEN THE TEETH
Battles were terrifying both for people and horses, and the simple snaffle bit rarely gave a rider suffcient control of his mount. A harsher curb bit, used with double reins, gave the rider more control.

Stirrups

SADDLEBAG
A horseman had to carry an assortment of spare clothing and equipment. This saddlebag, its ends decorated with the number of the horseman's regiment, was attached behind the saddle.

CARBINE
In 1811, French cuirassiers carried carbines. These guns were shorter than the infantry musket so as to be more handy on horseback, although in practice they were more useful for sentries and outposts than on the battlefield.

Buckle to attach saddlecloth to saddle

SADDLECLOTH
This saddlecloth was fitted over the horse's hindquarters behind the saddle and under the saddlebag. The grenade badges at its corners symbolize the elite nature of cuirassier regiments. The badge originated with grenadiers, traditionally the biggest and bravest of the infantry, who were trained to throw hand grenades. But it later denoted select troops in general.

CUIRASS
The steel of this Napoleonic French cuirassier's breastplate was strong enough to keep out musket balls and sword cuts. It was worn over the uniform jacket and held in place by the shoulder straps and a belt around the waist. The quilted lining protected the wearer from the edges of the metal.

Backplate

Leather shoulder strap, with brass protection

TUNIC AND TROUSERS
The tunic was made of closely woven material that kept the cold and rain out. The trousers were made of soft white hide, which was comfortable and hardwearing.

Heavy steel, protection against musket balls

Breastplate

Quilted lining

Cuffs decorated with regimental facing colors

Cartridge box for ammunition

BOOTS
Heavy leather boots gave some protection against the jostling that went on as men were pressed together in solid lines.

Feather plume for special occasions

Horsehair tuft

Fur turban

Leather chinstrap protected by brass scales

HELMET
A man's head presented a vulnerable target. A cuirassier's elaborate helmet had a steel skull, decorated with a fur turban. An embossed brass comb rose above it, with a long horsehair tail falling to the back, partly as ornament and partly to protect his neck. A small horsehair tuft decorated the front of the helmet. The red feather side-plume was initially worn all the time, but in 1808 the French army's 8th Regiment lost 85 in a single day, so plumes were thereafter worn only on special occasions.

Horsehair "mane"

Epaulets

Sword knot worn around the wrist to keep the sword safe

Brass-hilted sword with a straight, heavy blade; cuirassiers were trained to use the point whenever possible

FIGHTING WOMEN
Although women were usually discouraged from taking part in combat, a national emergency often broke down such taboos. These Serbian women were taught how to use rifles during a period of unrest in the Balkans.

THE BATTLEFIELD was a terrifying and deadly place. Soldiers had to balance a natural tendency to run away with the desire not to let down comrades and leaders. Soldiers were drilled to make them use their weapons efficiently, and to create a cohesive fighting unit with the discipline to withstand the shock of battle. Sometimes courage was promoted by a code of values that dominated an entire social class, like knights in medieval Europe or samurai in feudal Japan. But even the members of a warrior class needed training to form efficient armies rather than a collection of individual warriors.

Stringed bugle badge

Plume worn by officers, sergeants, and buglers

Cross-belt with whistle for giving orders

Sergeant's chevrons

Backsight: rifles had proper sights, which helped the rifleman aim

Officer's sash

READY, AIM, FIRE!
Some experienced soldiers argued that the aim of drill was to produce unquestioning obedience. King Frederick the Great (1713–86) of Prussia argued that "the common soldier must fear his officer more than the enemy." Others believed in a system founded on two-way trust and respect between officers and men. The British army's rifle regiments obeyed Pa philosophy that emphasized that "a Corps of Riflemen is expected to be one where intelligence is to distinguish every individual."

Hilt of sword bayonet

Cartridge box contains ammunition

Hessian boots (p. 17) worn with spurs by captains and higher ranks (these were mounted, even in infantry regiments)

Waxed canvas gaiters protect feet in wet weather

British riflemen demonstrate five different positions for firing the Baker rifle (pp. 42–43)

RIFLE DRILL
Drill books contained illustrations of soldiers carrying out the various parts of each drill movement. *The Rifle Manual and Firing Positions* (1804) shows how to "trail arms" from "shoulder arms." In the first part (left) the left hand was brought across the body to seize the rifle level with the shoulder. In the second (center) the right hand moved up to hold the rifle near its point of balance, and in the third (right) the left hand was removed, allowing the rifle to trail on the right side at arm's length.

HARDEE'S TACTICS
Drill books were written by officers who hoped to make money or enhance their reputations. These books became especially important when small armies grew rapidly and there were too few trained instructors. Hardee's *Tactics* was widely used by the largely amateur officers during the U.S. Civil War (1861–65).

SWORD EXERCISES
It was harder to train a cavalryman than an infantryman, for the former had to be able to ride and look after his horse as well as use his weapons. Cavalrymen, like these troopers, were taught sword drills, which consisted of a number of cuts, points (stabbing movements), and parries (blocking an opponent's sword cuts).

The sitting position was sometimes assumed on hillsides

Strap enabled gun to be carried over shoulder on march

British rifle regiments wore green rather than the red of the line infantry

Soldiers were taught to march in formation

13

Continued on next page

Drill and discipline

Efficient fire and movement depended on slick individual and group drill. Loading and firing drills were especially important, for they could enable one side to fire faster than the other. In the Napoleonic period well-drilled British infantry were able to fire faster than their opponents. Good drills also helped to avoid accidents: Marshal Gouvion St.-Cyr (1764–1830) reckoned that one quarter of French infantry casualties in the Napoleonic period were caused by soldiers being accidentally shot by men behind them. Drill, and emphasis on neatness and cleanliness, also helped to create a climate of disciplined obedience, in which the soldier would carry out orders instinctively. Finally, snappy drill and smart uniforms fostered a soldier's self-esteem, giving him pride and confidence in himself and his unit.

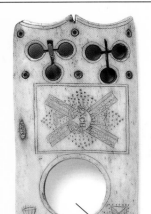

Hole for buttons

Name of owner's regiment

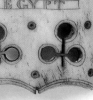

Regimental battle honor for the 1801 Egyptian campaign

MIGHTY RULER
Genghis Khan (1162–1227) led Mongol armies over huge tracts of Central Asia, China, and Russia. He was a skilled general and administrator, and his armies were not the undisciplined hordes of popular mythology, but well-organized bands of horsemen.

Button of 52nd Oxfordshire Regiment (Light Infantry)

BRIGHT AS A BUTTON
In peacetime, much time was devoted to keeping uniform and equipment clean and neat. Brass buttons had to be polished daily, and to keep the polish from staining the tunic, the soldier used a button stick. The buttons were inserted through the hole and then slid down the slot so that several could be polished at once.

KIT INSPECTION
This scene in a 19th-century British barracks would have been familiar to soldiers in most armies. Soldiers laid all their belongings out in a set manner ready for inspection. The officer would check that all items were present, clean, and in good condition.

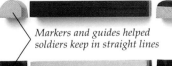

Markers and guides helped soldiers keep in straight lines

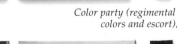

Color party (regimental colors and escort)

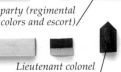

Lieutenant colonel (commanding officer)

Sergeant major

Junior major commands left wing of battalion

Adjutant (commanding officer's personal staff officer)

DRILL BLOCKS
Officers needed to know how to drill large bodies of men so that they could move companies (about 100 men) and battalions (about 800 men) from a marching column to the line of battle and not get them tangled up ("clubbed"). These military drill blocks, each of which represents an individual or a small group of men, enabled officers to practice drawing up units in various formations.

FORMING A SQUARE

There were times when drill was a matter of life and death. Infantrymen in a line were able to deliver the maximum volume of fire, but they were vulnerable to attack by charging cavalry. To meet this threat they formed squares, which were almost invulnerable to cavalry. The drill for forming a square had to be carried out quickly and without fuss.

ADVANCING IN A LINE

These soldiers were trained to march in a straight line in order to use their weapons effectively. They gained reassurance from the presence of comrades to left and right, and brave leadership by officers. The Scots Fusilier Guards (as they were then known) advancing toward the Russians at the Battle of the Alma (Crimean War, 1854–56).

Hinge, held by sergeant or sergeant major when stick was in use

Brass bar for adjusting size of pace

PACING IT OUT

To ensure that soldiers moved at the same speed, they were trained to take paces of uniform length and to take a set number of paces a minute. This pace stick, really a giant compass, is still used in the British army for measuring the length of paces.

Polished wood

End tipped with brass to make it more hardwearing

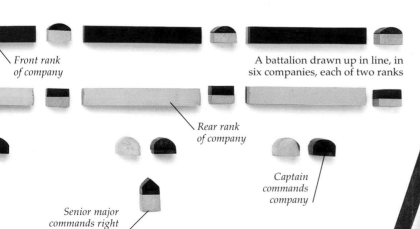

Front rank of company

A battalion drawn up in line, in six companies, each of two ranks

Rear rank of company

Captain commands company

Senior major commands right wing of battalion

Badges of rank

Aʀᴍɪᴇs ᴀʀᴇ ʟᴀʀɢᴇ and complex organizations, and can be run efficiently only if they have a clear chain of command. Badges of rank enable status to be recognized easily. They also helped to reinforce the military spirit by creating a climate of discipline and formality. There have always been many ways of indicating rank, such as the carrying of specific weapons or the wearing of more elaborate clothing by senior personnel. In the Chinese army, for example, senior mandarins wore tunics embroidered with particular symbols to denote their rank. Gradually, in the 19th century, most armies around the world began to indicate rank using distinctive badges worn on the sleeve, collar, or epaulet.

Shoulder cord worn by a field marshal

Shoulder cord worn by a colonel

Shoulder cord worn by a captain

Badge of a warrant officer class 1, worn on cuff

NCO's chevrons (sergeant), worn on sleeve

NCO's chevrons (corporal), worn on sleeve

ZULUS
In the Zulu army, officers were distinguished by leopard-skin kilts or capes and by certain types of blue feathers. In the 18th century, regiments were uniformly dressed. By the end of the 19th century, however, members of inexperienced regiments carried black shields, which they exchanged for white ones as their regiment's reputation grew.

Parchment leaf

BRITISH BADGES
Most armies make a distinction between commissioned officers, who hold a commission signed by the head of state or commander-in-chief; warrant officers, whose warrant of appointment carries a more junior status; and non-commissioned officers (NCOs), who can be appointed more easily. Over the past century, badges of rank worn on field uniforms have become increasingly inconspicuous to prevent leaders from being singled out by enemy marksmen.

JAPANESE FAN
The war fan was carried by Japanese officers in the time of the samurai as a mark of their rank. It could be used for signaling and, when closed, could parry (ward off) a sword cut or club an opponent. The fan itself was usually made of iron, covered with parchment decorated with the sun of Japan.

Iron sticks

THE THIN RED LINE
During the Crimean War battle of Balaclava (1854), Russian cavalry threatened the British base in Balaclava itself. The attack was thwarted by the "Thin Red Line" of the 93rd Sutherland Highlanders. The officer directing the fire shows his rank by wearing a sash and epaulets and carrying a sword. There is a corporal, with two chevrons, in the front rank, and a sergeant, with three chevrons, to the rear.

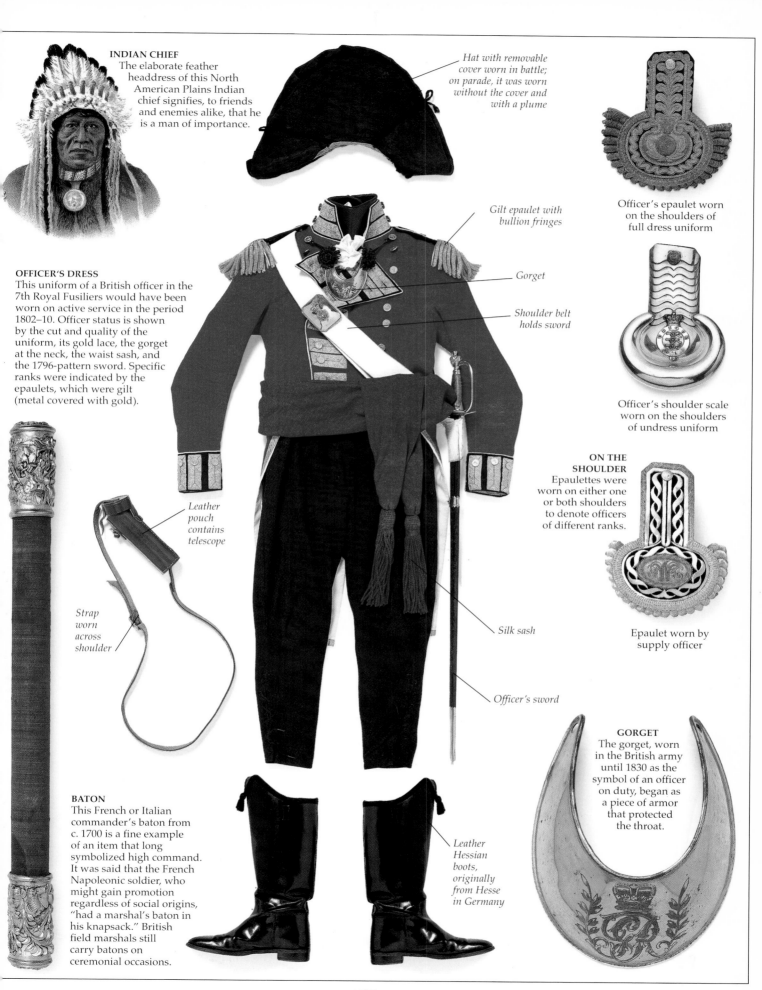

INDIAN CHIEF
The elaborate feather headdress of this North American Plains Indian chief signifies, to friends and enemies alike, that he is a man of importance.

Hat with removable cover worn in battle; on parade, it was worn without the cover and with a plume

Gilt epaulet with bullion fringes

Gorget

Shoulder belt holds sword

Officer's epaulet worn on the shoulders of full dress uniform

Officer's shoulder scale worn on the shoulders of undress uniform

OFFICER'S DRESS
This uniform of a British officer in the 7th Royal Fusiliers would have been worn on active service in the period 1802–10. Officer status is shown by the cut and quality of the uniform, its gold lace, the gorget at the neck, the waist sash, and the 1796-pattern sword. Specific ranks were indicated by the epaulets, which were gilt (metal covered with gold).

Leather pouch contains telescope

Strap worn across shoulder

Silk sash

ON THE SHOULDER
Epaulettes were worn on either one or both shoulders to denote officers of different ranks.

Epaulet worn by supply officer

Officer's sword

BATON
This French or Italian commander's baton from c. 1700 is a fine example of an item that long symbolized high command. It was said that the French Napoleonic soldier, who might gain promotion regardless of social origins, "had a marshal's baton in his knapsack." British field marshals still carry batons on ceremonial occasions.

Leather Hessian boots, originally from Hesse in Germany

GORGET
The gorget, worn in the British army until 1830 as the symbol of an officer on duty, began as a piece of armor that protected the throat.

Regimental colors

LIKE THE EAGLES CARRIED by Roman legions and the banners of medieval nobles, colors (flags) had both symbolic and practical importance. Symbolically, colors were the soul of a regiment – their loss in battle was a matter of deep disgrace. A British officer, whose regiment was in a desperate plight at Waterloo, felt relieved when he saw the "dear old rags" marched to safety. Practically, they enabled soldiers to recognize their units and rally to them in the confusion of battle. The color was regularly trooped through the ranks of a regiment so that men would recognize it.

COATS OF ARMS
Early colors often had items from the commanding officer's coat of arms. This shield, carried by King Matthias Corvinus of Hungary and Bohemia (c. 1443–90), bears his arms.

BATTLE HONORS
Glorious past achievements were marked in many ways. This British shabrack (officer's saddlecloth) is embroidered with battle honors for Dettingen (1743), the Peninsular War (1808–14), Waterloo (1815), Egypt (1882), and Tell el-Kebir (1882).

COLOR PARTY
The regimental color of the 9th East Norfolk Regiment is carried by an ensign, the most junior rank of commissioned officer, whose title is itself another word for flag. Behind him a color sergeant uses his short pike to defend the color. Ensigns were usually very young, and in close-quarter battle relied heavily on their color sergeants to defend them.

Silk matches facings (collars and cuffs) on uniforms

Colors usually supported in this belt

SYMBOL OF THE HUSSARS
French hussar standard, from the time of the republic in the late 18th century. This republican pattern was replaced by one with Napoleonic eagles. Hussars and other light cavalry, whose tasks demanded risk and isolation, did not always carry standards.

CHINESE COLORS
Here a Japanese officer is in the act of capturing a Chinese flag in the Sino-Japanese war over Korea (1894–95). The symbolism of colors was international.

Symbol of unity

BÉISSANCE ~ A LA LOI.

...LENTIA

HUSSARDS

Number indicates 7th Hussars

Troop symbols embroidered on silk ground

Latin inscription meaning "Second to None," a pun on the regimental number

NEC·SVNT·TIBI·MARTE·SECVND

Eagle held thunderbolt as a symbol of power

EAGLE
The Emperor Napoleon introduced the eagle as France's national symbol, and the eagles carried by French regiments consciously harked back to those of the Roman legions. This eagle of the French 105th Regiment of the Line was lost to the British at Waterloo in 1815.

FIGHT FOR THE STANDARD
Regimental colors inevitably became the center of fierce fighting as attackers sought to seize them from their bearers. Here Union and Confederate cavalrymen struggle for possession of a Confederate standard during the Civil War (1861–65). Men often risked their lives to protect their flag: at the Battle of Rezonville (Franco-Prussian War, 1870–71), the colors of the French 3rd Grenadiers of the Guard were passed from hand to hand as successive bearers were shot down. Eventually the regimental commander died, waving them and shouting, "To the color, my boys."

CAVALRY COLORS
Guidon of the 3rd Troop, 2nd Royal North British Dragoons, about 1780. This swallow-tailed guidon is typical of cavalry standards. For many years colors were carried by individual infantry companies or cavalry troops, but the practice generally died out in the 18th century.

Supply and transportation

LOGISTICS IS THE PRACTICAL ART of moving an army and keeping it supplied: there is much truth in the saying that "amateurs talk tactics, while professionals talk logistics." Until World War I, food for men and horses was an army's main requirement. Many commanders tried to live off the land by obtaining food from areas they crossed. But even the small armies of medieval Europe (some as small as 8,000 men) found this difficult. Armies also needed large numbers of horses. In 1700 an army of 60,000 men would have had about 40,000 horses. These would eat 500 tons (508 tonnes) of fodder a day. Inventions like the steam-driven train, gasoline-powered trucks, and canned food made things simpler. But at the same time improvements in weaponry increased the burden: by 1916 a British infantry division needed 20 railroad cars of food and 30 of ammunition every day.

INDIAN CAVALRY
Asian commanders, facing inhospitable terrain, and distances that dwarfed those in Europe, needed a firm grasp on logistics. The horse armies of antiquity – like the Magyars of Hungary, the Seljuk Turks, and the Mongols – were masters of rapid movement. These 18th-century cavalrymen from the northwest Indian state of Jaipur have bags of provisions hanging from their camels.

FRENCH TROOPS BOARDING
The railroad revolutionized war, enabling huge armies to be moved quickly and in a more organized way, with fewer accidents or desertions. In addition, soldiers and horses would be rested and fit to fight on arrival at the battlefield. In the Austro-Prussian War of 1866, the Prussians sent 200,000 men to the frontier with astonishing speed. In World War I (1914–18), so many of the Frenchmen who went to war by train in 1914 did not return that it was said that they had been "eaten by the Gare de l'Est."

SOYER OVEN
British army food was almost inedible during the Crimean War (1853–56). The great chef Alexis Soyer (1809–58) went out to help improve cooking. Here he is shown (on the left of the central group) with one of his specially designed ovens behind him.

THE RUSSIAN RAILROAD
The railroad was very valuable to large nations, or ones that, like Germany in World War I, had to face enemies on two sides. These Cossacks are being transported eastward on the Trans-Siberian Railroad to reinforce the Russian army fighting the Japanese in Manchuria during the Russo-Japanese War of 1904–5.

Saxon baggage wagon, used to transport provisions or camping equipment

Pair of horses attached here

BIVOUAC IN SPAIN

Moving armies could either be billeted (lodged with local inhabitants) or could bivouac in improvised, temporary open-air encampments. Bivouacking was essential in sparsely populated areas, and was a way of keeping men under better control. Here British soldiers are setting up a bivouac in Spain during the Peninsular War (1808–14).

TRAVELING FORGE

Horses required new horseshoes at regular intervals: in August 1914 one of the five German armies in France had 84,000 horses. This traveling forge was kept going even while the army marched, enabling blacksmiths to shoe horses or repair metalwork.

Part attached to horse

Bellows to fan fire

Lid lifts to give access to baggage

Large wheels were better on poor roads

Coals kept hot by being blown by bellows

FRENCH *VIVANDIERE*

Civilian merchants provided armies with many of their needs. French regiments had uniformed *vivandières* to sell comforts like bottles of brandy. This cartoon from the Crimean War shows a *vivandière* mocking the Russians.

SAXON BAGGAGE WAGON

Until transportation services became organized as a uniformed branch of the army in the 19th century, armies supplemented their own wagons with civilian vehicles and drivers when war broke out. This led to difficulties as drivers deserted and wagons broke down. Wagons built for military purposes were robust; this one was also small enough to be moved by soldiers if necessary. This wagon was used by the Saxon army in the late 18th century.

A soldier's pack

A SOLDIER'S LIFE ON THE ROAD involved weeks, sometimes months, of carrying spare clothing, water, cooking equipment, tools, and ammunition. Because stocking up on supplies was not always convenient, each man was responsible for carrying his own things for the duration of a campaign; experienced soldiers tended to jettison non-essential items. Equipment was often designed so that items not required in battle were kept in a backpack that could be removed before action, but this was not ideal because the victor would have to pause to recover his pack and the vanquished might lose his altogether.

Wool cloak

Mattock for digging ditches

Pack for personal items and three days' rations

Leather bottle for water or wine

Turf cutter for building turf ramparts

Shaft of javelin

ROMAN SOLDIER
A fully loaded legionary marched with a pack on his back in addition to his helmet, armor, shield, and weapons. The burden weighed 90 lb (40 kg) or more, and might have had to be carried up to 20 miles (32 km) a day.

String was doused with water to keep contents cool

A soldier kept his water bottle with him throughout his service

A PACK UNPACKED
Much of what a soldier carried, like spare clothing and cooking utensils, was government issue. A change of clothes, called fatigues, was included, and they were worn when off duty and for doing fatigues (chores) such as cleaning the mess. Many personal items, such as a razor and a shaving brush, were bought privately. No seasoned soldier wished to carry more than was necessary, but "home comforts" could make all the difference on campaigns in inhospitable places.

Camp kettle, used as a cooking pot as well as a plate

Bill hook for cutting food and chopping firewood

Shoe brush

Clothes brush

Soap

Straight-edged razor

Shaving bowl

Badger-hair shaving brush

Fork, knife, and spoon

Tin mug

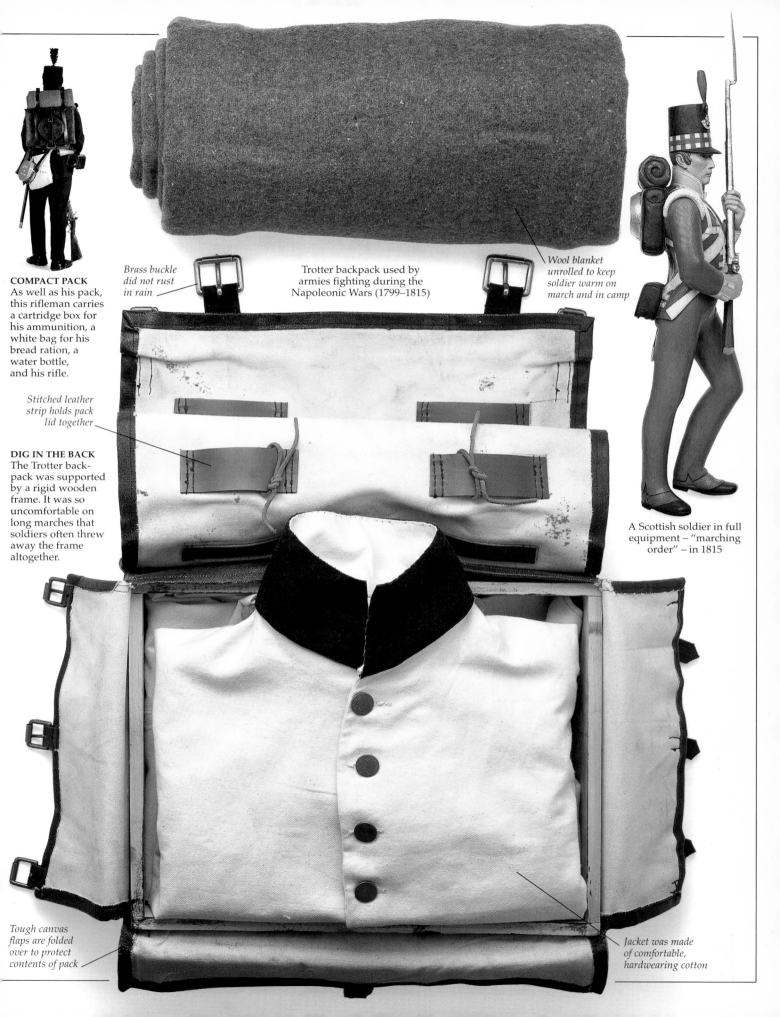

COMPACT PACK
As well as his pack, this rifleman carries a cartridge box for his ammunition, a white bag for his bread ration, a water bottle, and his rifle.

Brass buckle did not rust in rain

Trotter backpack used by armies fighting during the Napoleonic Wars (1799–1815)

Wool blanket unrolled to keep soldier warm on march and in camp

Stitched leather strip holds pack lid together

DIG IN THE BACK
The Trotter back-pack was supported by a rigid wooden frame. It was so uncomfortable on long marches that soldiers often threw away the frame altogether.

A Scottish soldier in full equipment – "marching order" – in 1815

Tough canvas flaps are folded over to protect contents of pack

Jacket was made of comfortable, hardwearing cotton

Reconnaissance

THE DUKE OF WELLINGTON (1769–1852), a British military commander, declared that the business of war consisted of finding out "what you don't know from what you do." Reconnaissance (surveying an area to gather information) is of fundamental importance. Without it, commanders cannot know the strength or location of hostile forces or the nature of the ground they wish to cross. They risk being taken by surprise, or advancing into country where an army will find it hard to move or to sustain itself. For centuries light cavalry, riding well ahead of the advancing columns, was the main means of reconnaissance, although it was also done on foot. With the development first of balloons and then aircraft, the "cavalry of the clouds" assumed growing importance, but even in the 20th century a mix of air and ground reconnaissance works best.

SABRETACHE
It is not easy for someone on a horse to keep writing materials accessible yet protected from the weather. So soldiers on reconnaissance, as well as others, wore a sabretache, which was in effect a field writing case. Inside it were compartments for pens, ink, and writing paper. The outer flap was usually decorated.

Emblem of French 8th Hussars

Sabretache hung on sword belt

COMPASS
This compass could be used both for verifying the direction of a march and for finding out the geographical location of distant places such as a house or a hill.

Lid to protect needle

Needle moves to show north

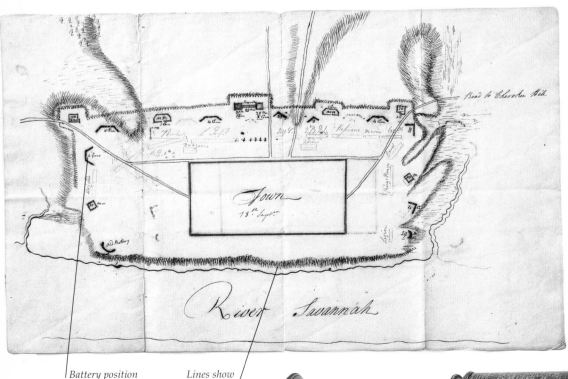

Road to Cherokee Hill

Town 18th Sept

River Savannah

Battery position for four guns

Lines show steep slope

SKETCH
This sketched map of the fortifications of Savannah, Georgia, was done by a Swiss officer in the British service during the Revolutionary War (1775–81). Officers needed to make an accurate record of information they acquired, and field sketching was widely taught at military academies.

TELESCOPE
For centuries commanders used the "perspective glass" (telescope) to observe enemy positions. This is a signaler's telescope, which enabled its user to read the enemy's flag or light signals in the distance.

Telescope retracts for storage

OBSERVATON BALLOON

On June 26, 1794, a French army met an allied Austro-German army at Fleurus, in Belgium. The French sent up a balloon, named *L'Entreprenant*, to hang over the battlefield, and observers sent messages sliding down its rope. However, these were of little value, and although the French won the battle, observation balloons fell out of favor until the Civil War (1861–65).

A view of the Battle of Fleurus painted on the lid of a snuff box

Strap to hang binoculars around neck when in use

RECONNAISSANCE AIRCRAFT

Military aircraft made their debut in 1911 when the Italians flew reconnaissance missions against the Turkish in Tripolitania (in Libya) and dropped some small bombs. Although air reconnaissance provided good information, pilots ran the risk of being shot down once they had been seen.

BROADER VIEW

Originally made from two telescopes joined together, binoculars were easier to use than a telescope. Although they did not usually produce the same degree of magnification, they generally gave a broader field of view. This pair of binoculars was presented by one officer to another officer who had saved his life.

Case to protect lenses when binoculars were not in use

HUSSAR PATROL

These British hussars of 1811 are typical of the light cavalry who played a key role in reconnaissance. They had to move discreetly to avoid being seen or heard by the enemy.

Field guns

FOR MUCH OF HISTORY, cannons were muzzleloaders (front-loading), firing solid cannonballs at a target well within view. Artillery emerged as the main casualty-producer of 20th-century battles. But this was only after technological advances, mostly in the 19th century, had produced breech-loading (rear-loading) weapons whose explosive shells were more deadly than either the roundshot or the primitive shells filled with black powder used by earlier guns.

Seats for gunners

Muzzle

Footrest

Bucket

CANNON
This British six-pounder of the mid-19th century shows the muzzleloading cannon at its peak. Its crew of five could fire a 6-lb (2.7-kg) ball to a maximum range of 3,300 yards (1,000 m) two or three times a minute.

Couplings attached the harnessed horses to the limber

Explosive shells

Fuse to explode shell

Bags containing gunpowder

LIMBER
The cannon was towed directly behind its limber, whose chest contained sufficient ammunition to keep the gun supplied for some time. Ammunition wagons (caissons) would be used to replenish limbers if ammunition ran short. The limber also carried tools to help the detachment to prepare the gun's position. The six-horse team pulling this gun was attached to the couplings.

Tools are stored on the back of the limber

Cannon attached to limber during transport

Ammunition chests are safely locked during transport

ASSEMBLING
When mounting a gun, the barrel required skilled handling. The barrel of a light six-pounder weighed 670 lb (305 kg).

EARLY CANNON
Simple cannon from around 1400 caused few casualties but could terrify both horses and new soldiers.

FUENTES DE ONORO
Horse artillery, with all gunners on horseback, was intended to keep pace with cavalry. At the Battle of Fuentes de Oñoro (Spain, 1811) an English horse artillery battery was surrounded by French cavalry, but the English charged right through the enemy horsemen to escape.

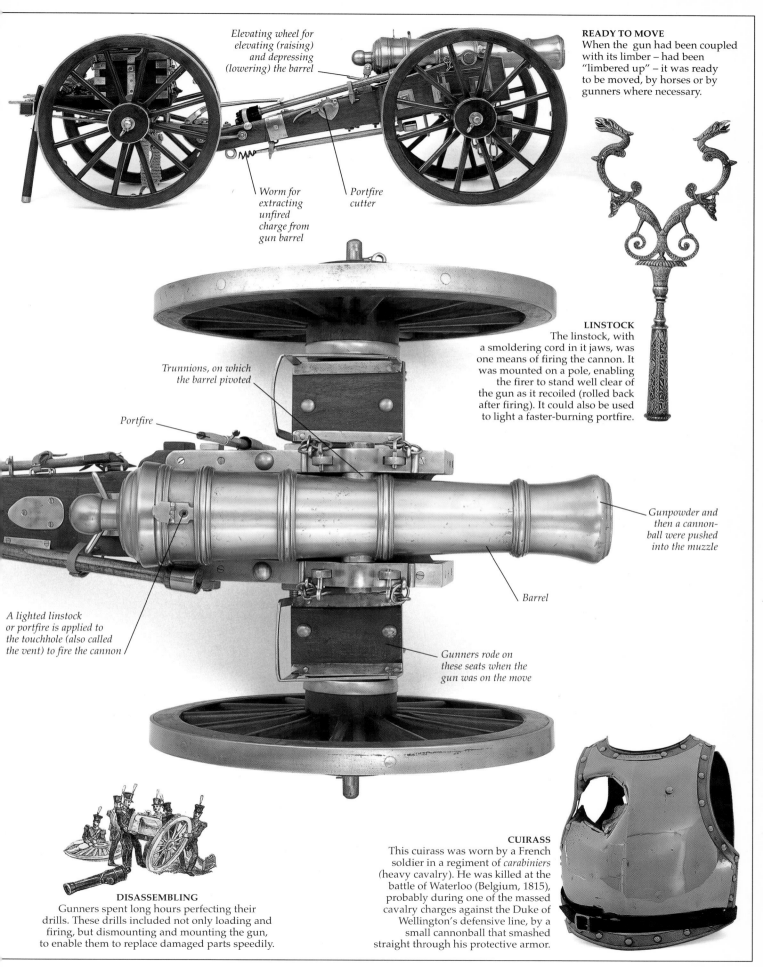

Elevating wheel for elevating (raising) and depressing (lowering) the barrel

Worm for extracting unfired charge from gun barrel

Portfire cutter

READY TO MOVE
When the gun had been coupled with its limber – had been "limbered up" – it was ready to be moved, by horses or by gunners where necessary.

Trunnions, on which the barrel pivoted

Portfire

LINSTOCK
The linstock, with a smoldering cord in it jaws, was one means of firing the cannon. It was mounted on a pole, enabling the firer to stand well clear of the gun as it recoiled (rolled back after firing). It could also be used to light a faster-burning portfire.

Gunpowder and then a cannon-ball were pushed into the muzzle

A lighted linstock or portfire is applied to the touchhole (also called the vent) to fire the cannon

Barrel

Gunners rode on these seats when the gun was on the move

DISASSEMBLING
Gunners spent long hours perfecting their drills. These drills included not only loading and firing, but dismounting and mounting the gun, to enable them to replace damaged parts speedily.

CUIRASS
This cuirass was worn by a French soldier in a regiment of *carabiniers* (heavy cavalry). He was killed at the battle of Waterloo (Belgium, 1815), probably during one of the massed cavalry charges against the Duke of Wellington's defensive line, by a small cannonball that smashed straight through his protective armor.

Continued on next page

Serving the guns

The detachment of men who operated cannon and mortars needed to be expert at loading and firing. Practice drills helped men to keep up a rapid rate of fire, prevent mistakes, and remain effective despite enemy fire. Muzzleloading cannon were loaded with gunpowder, usually in bagged charges. The bag was rammed home; it was followed with a projectile, which could be a solid ball, explosive shell, or some form of multiple shot. Early cannon were fired by lighting fine priming powder sprinkled into the touchhole. Later a friction primer was inserted into the vent and fired by pulling a cord called a lanyard.

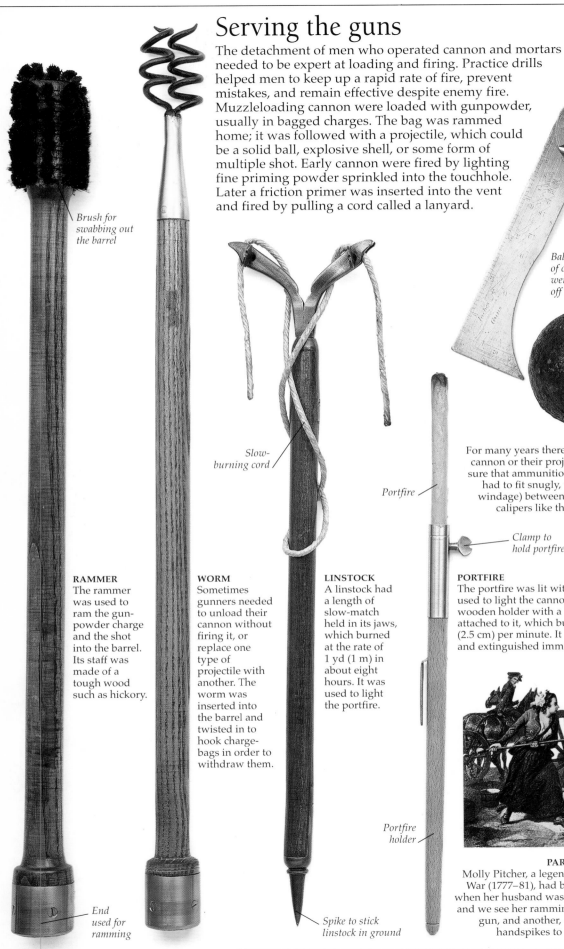

Brush for swabbing out the barrel

Slow-burning cord

Portfire

Arms can be straightened out to make a ruler

Ball fits into arms of calipers so that weight can be read off calibrations

CALIPERS
For many years there was no proper standardization of cannon or their projectiles, and gunners needed to be sure that ammunition was the right size. A cannonball had to fit snugly, with just a little gap (known as windage) between it and the barrel. Gunners used calipers like these to measure cannonballs.

Clamp to hold portfire

PORTFIRE
The portfire was lit with the linstock and was used to light the cannon. This portfire had a wooden holder with a length of quick burner attached to it, which burned at the rate of 1 in (2.5 cm) per minute. It was lit to fire the cannon and extinguished immediately afterward.

RAMMER
The rammer was used to ram the gunpowder charge and the shot into the barrel. Its staff was made of a tough wood such as hickory.

WORM
Sometimes gunners needed to unload their cannon without firing it, or replace one type of projectile with another. The worm was inserted into the barrel and twisted in to hook charge-bags in order to withdraw them.

LINSTOCK
A linstock had a length of slow-match held in its jaws, which burned at the rate of 1 yd (1 m) in about eight hours. It was used to light the portfire.

Portfire holder

PART OF THE CREW
Molly Pitcher, a legendary heroine of the Revolutionary War (1777–81), had been taking water to men in battle when her husband was killed at his gun. She took his place and we see her ramming while one gunner lays (aims) the gun, and another, acting on his instructions, uses handspikes to swing the weapon around.

End used for ramming

Spike to stick linstock in ground

FLAMING SHOT
Although solid shot was most common, other projectiles were available. This experimental roundshot was intended to have inflammable material in it to set fire to buildings, for example.

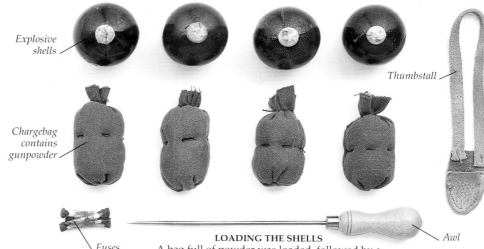

Explosive shells

Thumbstall

Chargebag contains gunpowder

Fuses

Awl

LOADING THE SHELLS
A bag full of powder was loaded, followed by a solid shot or an explosive shell. A long awl was thrust through the vent to enable a fuse or fine priming powder to enter the bagged charge. The thumbstall was held over the vent when a gun was swabbed out after firing, to prevent a draft, which could light smoldering debris left by the chargebag.

GRAPESHOT
Multiple shot, such as grapeshot, shown here, or canister (a container of musket balls), split up on leaving the gun's muzzle. It was murderous at close range.

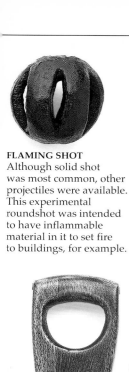

PICK
An assortment of tools were carried, usually on the cannon's limber. The pick enabled gunners to break up the ground when they needed to.

GUN BEING FIRED
British gunners are here shown firing one of the last muzzleloading cannon in British service. Breech-loading cannon were successfully used by the Germans in the Franco-Prussian War (1870–71), and most other nations soon introduced them. The gunners stood clear to avoid injury when the gun jumped back on recoil.

SHOVEL
If gunners had time, they could make their task easier by sloping the earth beneath the gun so that it would naturally roll back into the firing position after recoil.

AX
The ax enabled gunners to cut away roots or branches in the way.

BUCKET
Water was essential for loading, as gunners needed to swab the barrel after firing to ensure that no sparks remained to ignite the next powder charge inserted, and to help remove fouling (the remnants of burned powder).

Rapid-fire weapons

TRADITIONAL WEAPONS had to be laboriously loaded each time they were fired, so inventors experimented with multi-barreled guns to increase the rate of fire. However, it was not until the mid-19th century that reliable rapid-fire weapons were produced. The Gatling gun, patented by Dr. Richard Gatling (1818–1903), had a number of barrels, most often 10. As they were cranked around by hand, each was fed with a cartridge and fired. A few Gatling guns saw service in the Civil War (1861–65), but the weapon was used throughout the world by the 1870s. The French army adopted the *mitrailleuse* in 1865. Its barrels remained stationary. A loading plate filled with ammunition was inserted into the breech, and the operator turned the firing crank to fire each barrel in turn.

MITRAILLEUSE
The *mitrailleuse*, whose name literally means "grapeshot shooter", had a maximum effective range of 1,640 yd (1,500 m) against a large target. A gunner inserts a loaded firing plate.

AMMUNITION
The development of cartridges whose gunpowder was contained in sturdy brass or copper cases made possible the development of rapid-fire weapons. Both the *mitrailleuse* and the Gatling gun could fire special cartridges containing several bullets. Shown above is a buckshot round for the Gatling.

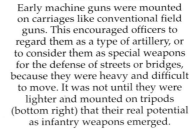

Crank to turn barrels

Magazine contained cartridges and fed them into the barrel as they were needed

Barrel

Crank

Ammunition fired from these holes

Elevating gear for elevating (raising) and depressing (lowering) the barrels

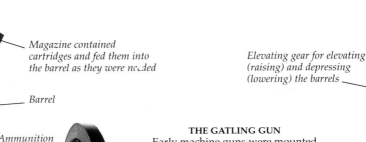

THE GATLING GUN
Early machine guns were mounted on carriages like conventional field guns. This encouraged officers to regard them as a type of artillery, or to consider them as special weapons for the defense of streets or bridges, because they were heavy and difficult to move. It was not until they were lighter and mounted on tripods (bottom right) that their real potential as infantry weapons emerged.

Axle

Ring to take handspike to swing gun left and right

Trail enabled the gun to be towed and provided a prop when it was in use

Magazine with ammunition; this version of the Gatling, used by the British in India and Africa, took 1-in- (2.5-cm-) caliber cartidges

FRANCO-PRUSSIAN WAR
In the Franco-Prussian War of 1870–71 the French failed to use the *mitrailleuse* to its best effect, keeping it back with the field guns rather than pushing it forward with the infantry. As a consequence, it was usually knocked out by superior German cannon. Because development had been secret, few officers and men knew how it worked, and its mechanism was so fragile that untrained men often broke it.

Foresight

Pivot for revolving mechanism

Barrels

THE BUSINESS END
Gatling guns were made in several calibers between .45 in (1 cm) and 1 in (2.5 cm). Most had 10 barrels, which could be cranked fast enough to fire 1,000 rounds a minute.

Dr. Gatling in 1893, with his light gun equipped with a drum magazine

Shackle for attaching rope helped gunners move gun on difficult ground

High-angle fire

A CANNON REACHES MAXIMUM RANGE with its barrel at an angle of 45 degrees. Above this level the weapon is said to be firing at a high angle; low-angle fire is below 45 degrees. Mortars were short and stubby, and were specifically designed for high-angle fire. They fired bombs (explosive shells) when most guns fired only solid balls; they were used in sieges because their projectiles would pass over fortifications to burst inside the town or fortress. Howitzers were longer-barreled and could fire at low or high angles. Like mortars, they used shells when these were uncommon in cannons. Mortars and howitzers remained important because they could fire over ridges and drop shells into sheltered ground or trench systems. Small "trench mortars" were widely used in World War I (1914–18).

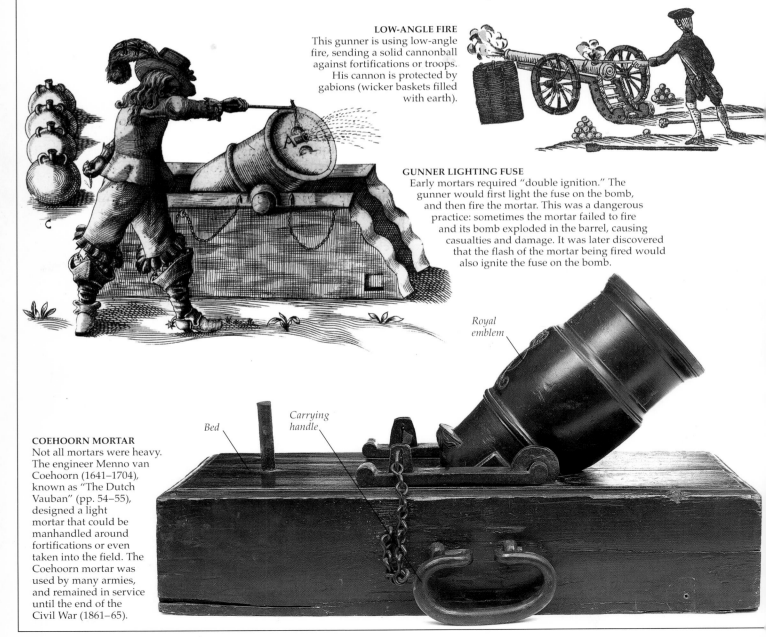

FIRING UP
From his mortar, the gunner fires an explosive bomb over fortifications. Cannon and mortars caused a revolution in fortress design. The high stone walls that had characterized medieval fortification offered easy targets. They were replaced by low, squat "artillery fortifications" that were much harder to damage. Important buildings, like ammunition warehouses, were built with strong roofs covered with earth to make them "bomb-proof" – able to resist mortar bombs.

LOW-ANGLE FIRE
This gunner is using low-angle fire, sending a solid cannonball against fortifications or troops. His cannon is protected by gabions (wicker baskets filled with earth).

GUNNER LIGHTING FUSE
Early mortars required "double ignition." The gunner would first light the fuse on the bomb, and then fire the mortar. This was a dangerous practice: sometimes the mortar failed to fire and its bomb exploded in the barrel, causing casualties and damage. It was later discovered that the flash of the mortar being fired would also ignite the fuse on the bomb.

Royal emblem

Bed

Carrying handle

COEHOORN MORTAR
Not all mortars were heavy. The engineer Menno van Coehoorn (1641–1704), known as "The Dutch Vauban" (pp. 54–55), designed a light mortar that could be manhandled around fortifications or even taken into the field. The Coehoorn mortar was used by many armies, and remained in service until the end of the Civil War (1861–65).

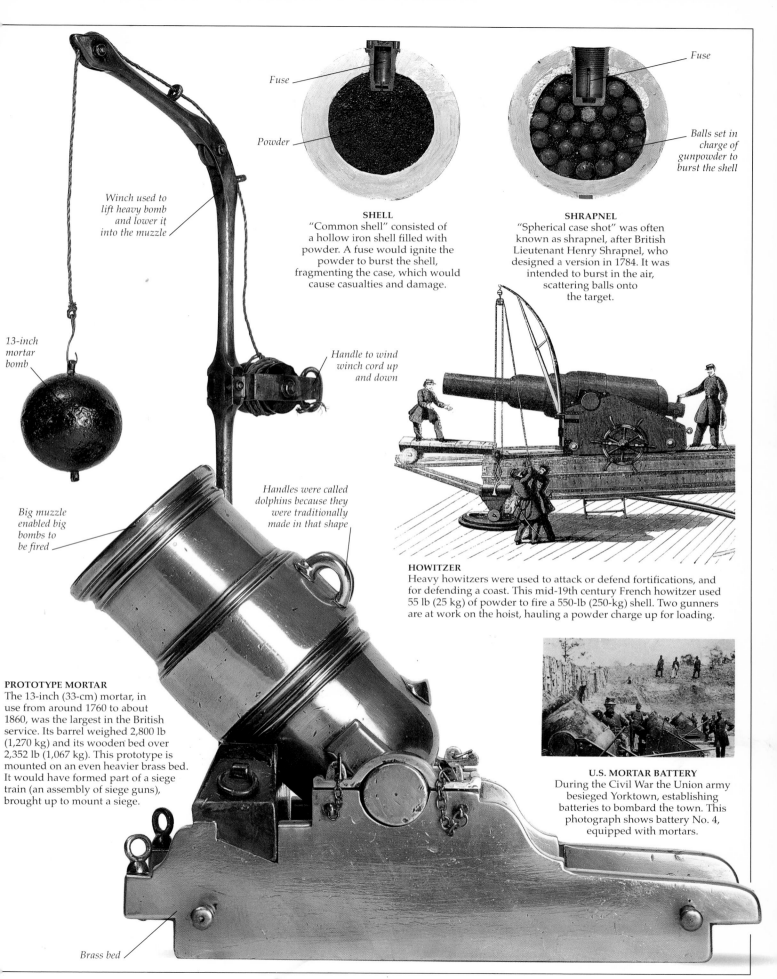

Winch used to lift heavy bomb and lower it into the muzzle

Handle to wind winch cord up and down

13-inch mortar bomb

Fuse

Powder

SHELL
"Common shell" consisted of a hollow iron shell filled with powder. A fuse would ignite the powder to burst the shell, fragmenting the case, which would cause casualties and damage.

Fuse

Balls set in charge of gunpowder to burst the shell

SHRAPNEL
"Spherical case shot" was often known as shrapnel, after British Lieutenant Henry Shrapnel, who designed a version in 1784. It was intended to burst in the air, scattering balls onto the target.

Big muzzle enabled big bombs to be fired

Handles were called dolphins because they were traditionally made in that shape

HOWITZER
Heavy howitzers were used to attack or defend fortifications, and for defending a coast. This mid-19th century French howitzer used 55 lb (25 kg) of powder to fire a 550-lb (250-kg) shell. Two gunners are at work on the hoist, hauling a powder charge up for loading.

PROTOTYPE MORTAR
The 13-inch (33-cm) mortar, in use from around 1760 to about 1860, was the largest in the British service. Its barrel weighed 2,800 lb (1,270 kg) and its wooden bed over 2,352 lb (1,067 kg). This prototype is mounted on an even heavier brass bed. It would have formed part of a siege train (an assembly of siege guns), brought up to mount a siege.

U.S. MORTAR BATTERY
During the Civil War the Union army besieged Yorktown, establishing batteries to bombard the town. This photograph shows battery No. 4, equipped with mortars.

Brass bed

Artillery instruments

EARLY CANNON WERE CUMBERSOME and inaccurate. Prussian gunners maintained that "the first shot is for God, the second is for the devil, and only the third is for the king." In the earliest textbook on gunnery (1537), Niccolo Tartaglia described the relationship between the speed of the cannonball and the path it followed, writing "the more swift the pellet doth fly, the less crooked is its range." To make the most of their cannon, gunners needed instruments to position them correctly. They used quadrants to find the angle of elevation and calculate how far a shot would go. Rulers enabled them to measure a cannon's muzzle to establish the weight of ball it fired, levels helped them to place guns precisely upright, and they used dividers to measure ranges on maps.

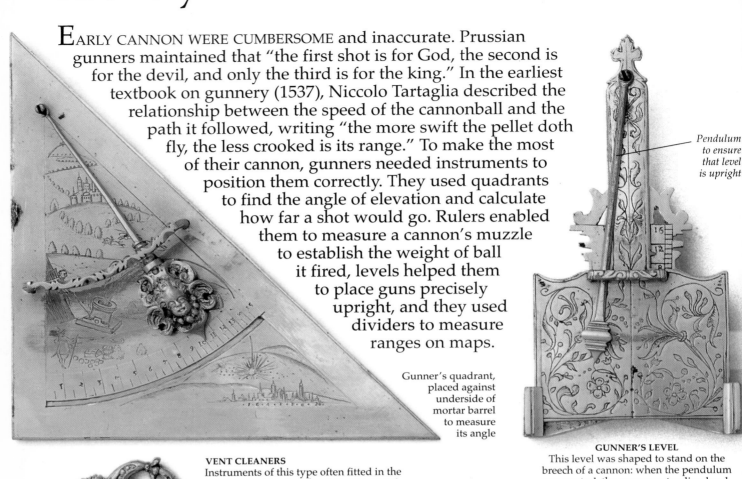

Pendulum to ensure that level is upright

Gunner's quadrant, placed against underside of mortar barrel to measure its angle

GUNNER'S LEVEL
This level was shaped to stand on the breech of a cannon: when the pendulum was central, the gun was standing level.

VENT CLEANERS
Instruments of this type often fitted in the scabbard of the elaborate sword sometimes carried by master gunners.

Studs protect the pole from wear, as well as holding the quadrant in place

Label shows which type of shot the scale is for – in this case, gravel

SLA

UP, UP, AND AWAY!
This fanciful engraving of 1789 shows a mortar firing a large bomb and several smaller ones. Mortars could fire multiple projectiles, but they were usually the same size, and it was difficult to ensure that all ignited properly.

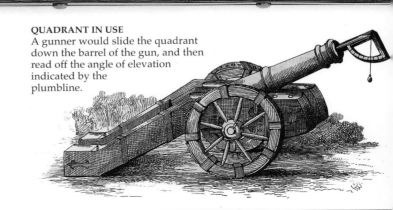

QUADRANT IN USE
A gunner would slide the quadrant down the barrel of the gun, and then read off the angle of elevation indicated by the plumbline.

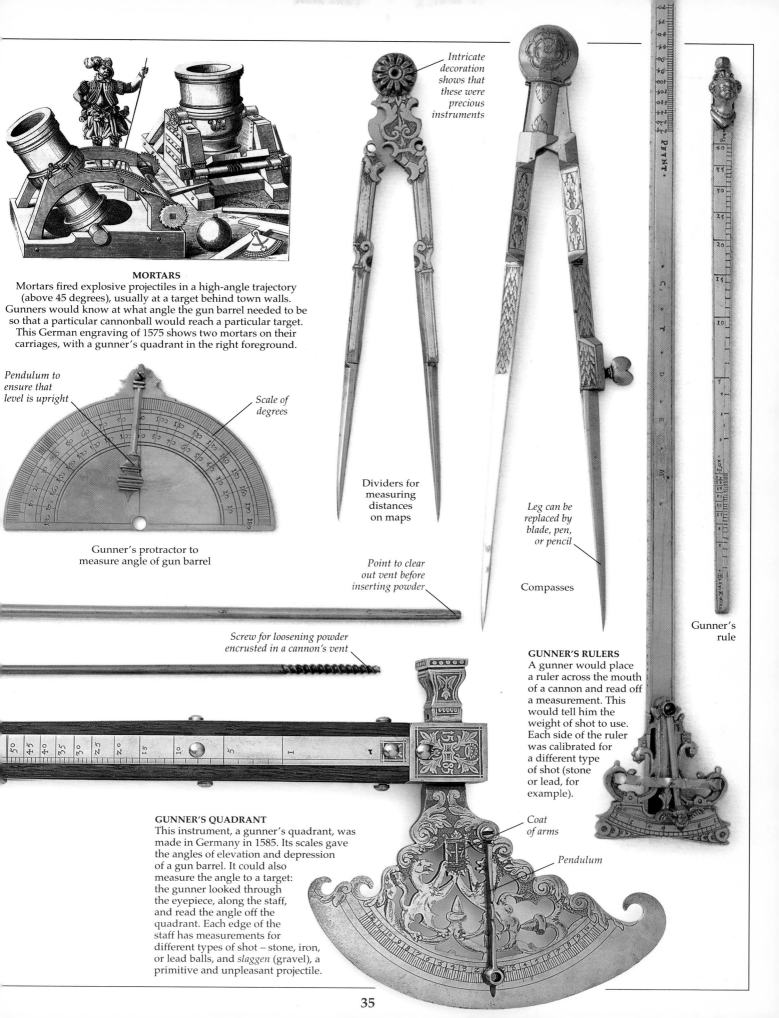

MORTARS

Mortars fired explosive projectiles in a high-angle trajectory (above 45 degrees), usually at a target behind town walls. Gunners would know at what angle the gun barrel needed to be so that a particular cannonball would reach a particular target. This German engraving of 1575 shows two mortars on their carriages, with a gunner's quadrant in the right foreground.

Pendulum to ensure that level is upright

Scale of degrees

Gunner's protractor to measure angle of gun barrel

Intricate decoration shows that these were precious instruments

Dividers for measuring distances on maps

Leg can be replaced by blade, pen, or pencil

Compasses

Gunner's rule

Point to clear out vent before inserting powder

Screw for loosening powder encrusted in a cannon's vent

GUNNER'S RULERS

A gunner would place a ruler across the mouth of a cannon and read off a measurement. This would tell him the weight of shot to use. Each side of the ruler was calibrated for a different type of shot (stone or lead, for example).

Coat of arms

Pendulum

GUNNER'S QUADRANT

This instrument, a gunner's quadrant, was made in Germany in 1585. Its scales gave the angles of elevation and depression of a gun barrel. It could also measure the angle to a target: the gunner looked through the eyepiece, along the staff, and read the angle off the quadrant. Each edge of the staff has measurements for different types of shot – stone, iron, or lead balls, and *slaggen* (gravel), a primitive and unpleasant projectile.

Bows and arrows

WEAPONS THAT WERE FIRED and thrown enabled their users to attack an opponent from a distance. Bows played a major role in battle. The longbow, made of wood or a combination of materials like wood and horn, was deadly in skilled hands and could even send its arrow through some types of armor. However, it took years of practice to use one effectively. The crossbow was more powerful than the longbow, but it was heavier and had a slower rate of fire. Both longbow and crossbow were used in medieval Europe. Thrown weapons such as javelins (throwing spears) were used by people all over the world, including Romans, African peoples, and Aboriginal peoples of Australia. Hand grenades came into use in the 17th century, and did more damage than other thrown weapons by exploding on impact.

FIREWORKS
Arrows tipped with inflammable compounds could be shot into wooden buildings or on to thatched roofs to cause fires. These 17th-century illustrations (above and right) show slightly fanciful versions of flaming arrows.

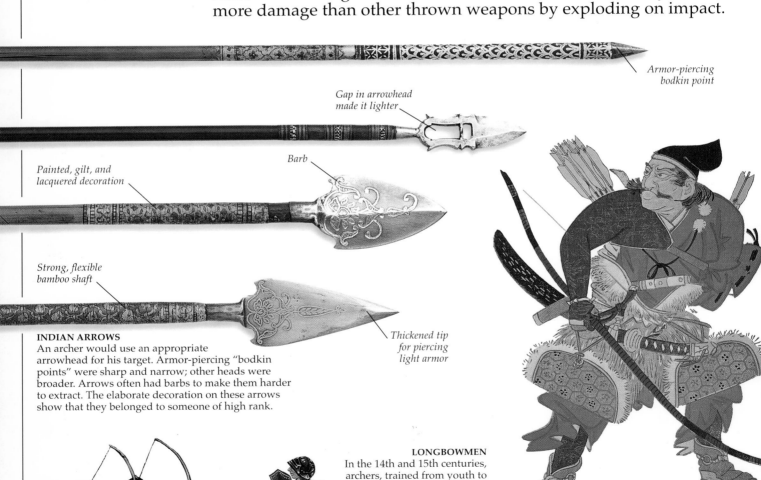

Armor-piercing bodkin point

Gap in arrowhead made it lighter

Barb

Painted, gilt, and lacquered decoration

Strong, flexible bamboo shaft

Thickened tip for piercing light armor

INDIAN ARROWS
An archer would use an appropriate arrowhead for his target. Armor-piercing "bodkin points" were sharp and narrow; other heads were broader. Arrows often had barbs to make them harder to extract. The elaborate decoration on these arrows show that they belonged to someone of high rank.

LONGBOWMEN
In the 14th and 15th centuries, archers, trained from youth to use the longbow, were the prime instrument of English victory over the French in battles in the Hundred Years War (1337–1453) like Crécy, Poitiers, and Agincourt. This was mainly because French knights, used to hand-to-hand combat, were killed by the longbowmen as they charged toward successive hails of arrows.

JAPANESE ARCHER
Japanese war bows were made of bamboo and other wood combined, and were longer than European longbows. Whereas a European knight would have considered it beneath his dignity to use a bow in battle, many samurai were skilled archers. They were trained from childhood to follow a strict code called the "warrior's way," and were prepared to fight to death for their overlord.

CROSSBOW

The crossbow was popular in medieval Europe, and versions were used in China and Japan. In some lighter models the string was drawn back by means of a hook called a goat's-foot lever. Usually the bow was so powerful that its user needed a small winch, called a moulinet, to draw it. When the bow was drawn, the moulinet was removed and the bolt was loaded. The crossbow was powerful and accurate, but it was slow to load and hard to protect from rain or damp. At Crécy (1346) the Genoese crossbowmen on the French side were outshot by English longbowmen.

BOOMERANG

The boomerang is a curved throwing stick used for fighting or hunting by the Aboriginal peoples of Australia. Although some boomerangs were specially designed to return to the thrower, many were not. Similar weapons were used in Africa and India.

Bowstring

Crossbow bolt with broad head, used for battles and hunting

Groove for bolt

Crossbow bolt with steel armor-piercing tip

Hand grenade

Hook hooked over bowstring, so that it could be drawn back

NORTH BRITISH GRENADIER

The hand grenade was used in the 17th and 18th centuries when fortifications were attacked. Grenadiers wore a cap that made it easy for them to sling their musket over their shoulder, leaving both hands free. They used a length of smoldering cord (the match) to light the fuse on the grenade, an iron sphere filled with powder, before throwing it.

CROSSBOWMEN

These crossbowmen are in action during the successful siege of Jerusalem by the Crusaders in 1099. While his companions fire, the soldier on the right is reloading his bow, putting one foot through the stirrup to hold it down and using the moulinet to wind back the string. Crossbowmen and archers sometimes worked in pairs, with one reloading behind a shield while the other fired.

Windlass handle

Base of crossbow fitted into windlass

Maces and battle-axes

WIDELY USED BY KNIGHTS and warriors from the 11th to the 16th centuries, maces and battle-axes could be used to smash their way through helmets and body armor as well as chain mail. While armor offered good protection against edged weapons like swords or spears, some daggers were specially designed to defeat armor by penetrating where plates joined. It could be difficult to kill a dismounted knight if the right weapon was not at hand. At the battle of Bouvines, fought in 1214 near Lille in northern France, the French King Philip Augustus was surrounded by enemy footsoldiers, but they failed to kill him before help arrived.

Armor-piercing spike

Flange

Long handle gave the user extra "swing"

SPIKED MACE
Helmets were often designed to encourage blows to glance off them. This 18th-century Indian mace is embellished with spikes that would prevent it from slipping when it struck. Cruder spiked weapons – called "morning stars" or "holy water sprinklers" – were used in Europe.

Grip

Top of handle protects hand

Weighted head helped the user to strike harder

Hammer head

Spike for penetrating armor

WAR HAMMER
The war hammer was a popular weapon in Europe. It usually had a sharp point at the back, and a blunt head or a set of claws, which could pierce armor, at the front. This specimen is Polish or Hungarian and dates from about 1700.

Ornamental studs

FLANGED MACE
This mace, made in Italy in about 1550, has the weight to smash armor, and flanges that help it to penetrate the armor. Maces were often hung from a knight's saddle when not in use. They were sometimes carried by fighting clerics (churchmen), who were forbidden to shed blood!

WARRIOR MONK
Most Japanese warriors carried a two-handed sword that had a sharp, heavy blade. However, this formidable warrior monk is armed with a mighty club. These monks wore a mixture of military and monkish dress, with a cap instead of a helmet.

PUNCHING DAGGER
This Indian dagger, called a katar, was held by the grip that runs at right angles to the blade, so that the blow was delivered by punching. This late-18th-century version has a double blade, but single blades with reinforced points for the penetration of armor were more common.

Wristguard

Grip

Serrated blades caused more damage to armor and opponent

Armor-piercing points

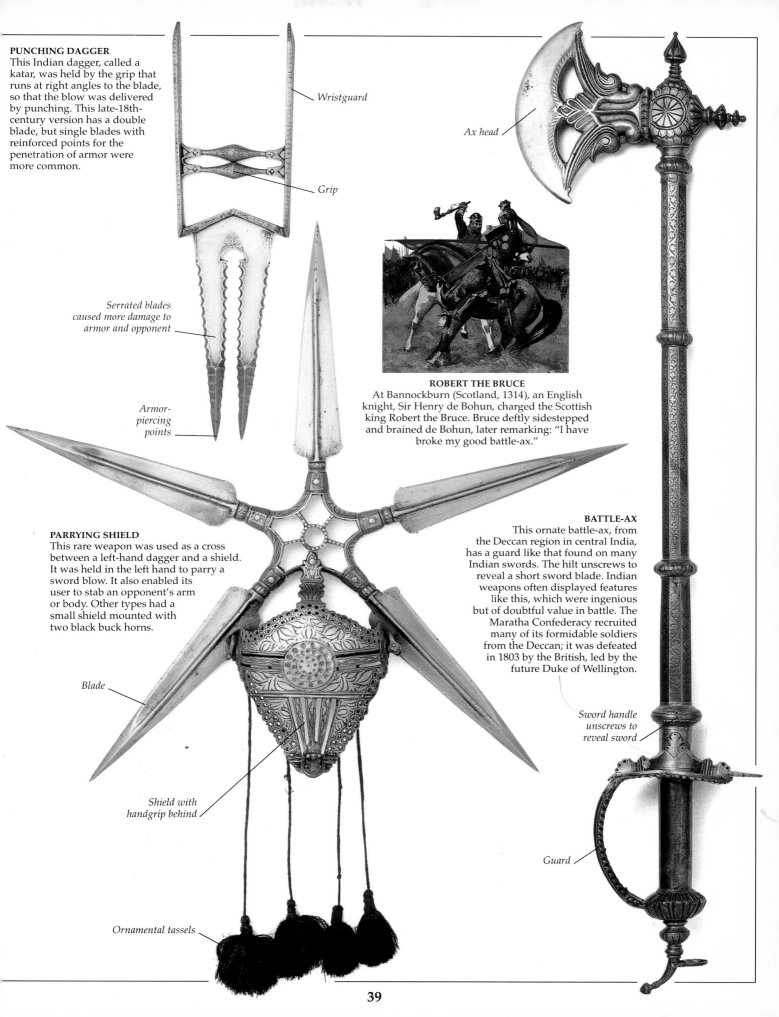

ROBERT THE BRUCE
At Bannockburn (Scotland, 1314), an English knight, Sir Henry de Bohun, charged the Scottish king Robert the Bruce. Bruce deftly sidestepped and brained de Bohun, later remarking: "I have broke my good battle-ax."

Ax head

PARRYING SHIELD
This rare weapon was used as a cross between a left-hand dagger and a shield. It was held in the left hand to parry a sword blow. It also enabled its user to stab an opponent's arm or body. Other types had a small shield mounted with two black buck horns.

Blade

Shield with handgrip behind

Ornamental tassels

BATTLE-AX
This ornate battle-ax, from the Deccan region in central India, has a guard like that found on many Indian swords. The hilt unscrews to reveal a short sword blade. Indian weapons often displayed features like this, which were ingenious but of doubtful value in battle. The Maratha Confederacy recruited many of its formidable soldiers from the Deccan; it was defeated in 1803 by the British, led by the future Duke of Wellington.

Sword handle unscrews to reveal sword

Guard

Swords

THE SWORD WAS USED in prehistoric times, and was still carried by cavalrymen as late as the end of World War I (1914–18). There were two main types of swords. Cutting swords, such as a medieval knight's cross-hilted sword or a Highland officer's broadsword, had heavy blades with sharp edges. Stabbing swords, like the rapier, were lighter and had sharp points. Many military swords were general purpose "cut and thrust" weapons. Real damage in battle was usually done by well-directed thrusts, which produced lethal wounds, rather than by cuts, which were often deflected by an opponent's helmet.

Hand and wrist fit inside steel gauntlet, which is held by a grip inside

SWORD DRILL
To use his sword effectively, a soldier had to know how to attack his enemy, and to protect himself by parries (defensive strokes). This series of illustrations comes from an early-19th-century British drill book and shows exercises for the broadsword.

LADIES FIGHTING
This 15th-century lady is wielding a knightly broadsword. Although women rarely took up arms in medieval Europe, in Japan women of samurai families were sometimes trained to use a light halberd (p. 45).

SWORD-BREAKER
When men fought on foot with rapiers, they often carried a dagger in the left hand. A sword-breaker was also carried in the left hand, and its serrated edge was intended to catch an opponent's blade, which could then be broken with a twist of the wrist. It could also be used as a conventional dagger. This example was made in Italy in about 1660.

GAUNTLET SWORD
A fighter's sword hand and forearm were in danger from an opponent's cuts. This 17th-century Indian gauntlet sword embodied protection for the hand and the wrist. Its blade was made in Solingen, a center of sword production in Germany. Good-quality European blades were often used in Asia, and vice versa; attractively patterned "Damascus" blades are sometimes found on 19th-century European swords.

Barbs to trap opponent's blade

Sharp edge

Solingen maker's mark

Broad, double-edged blade

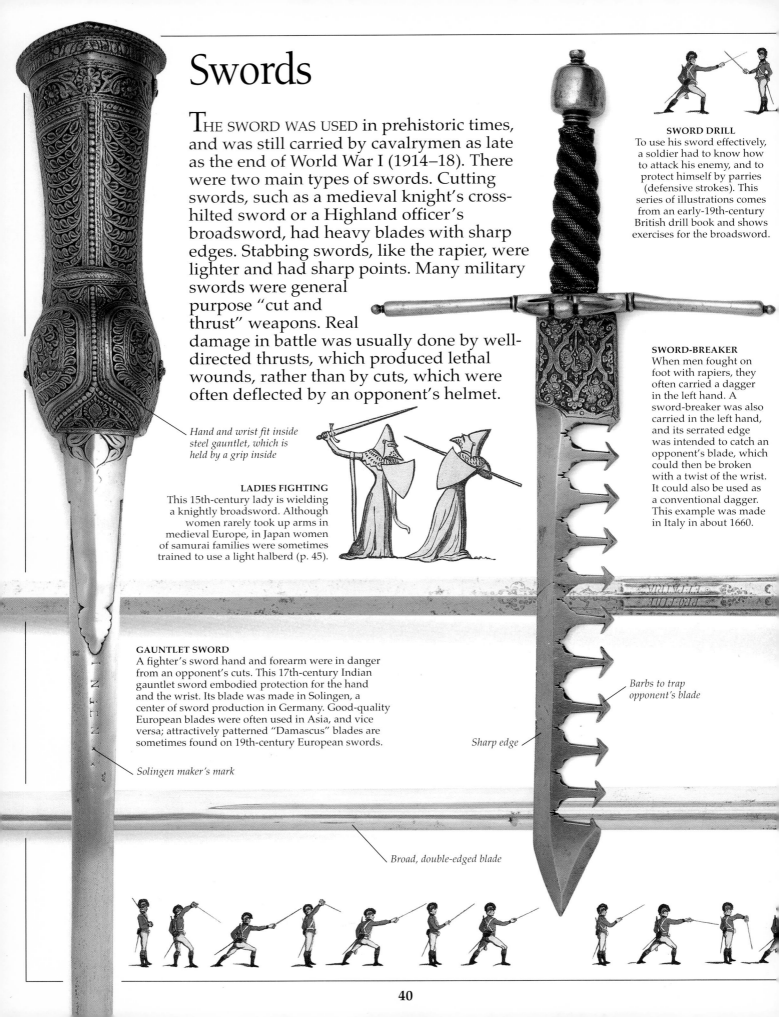

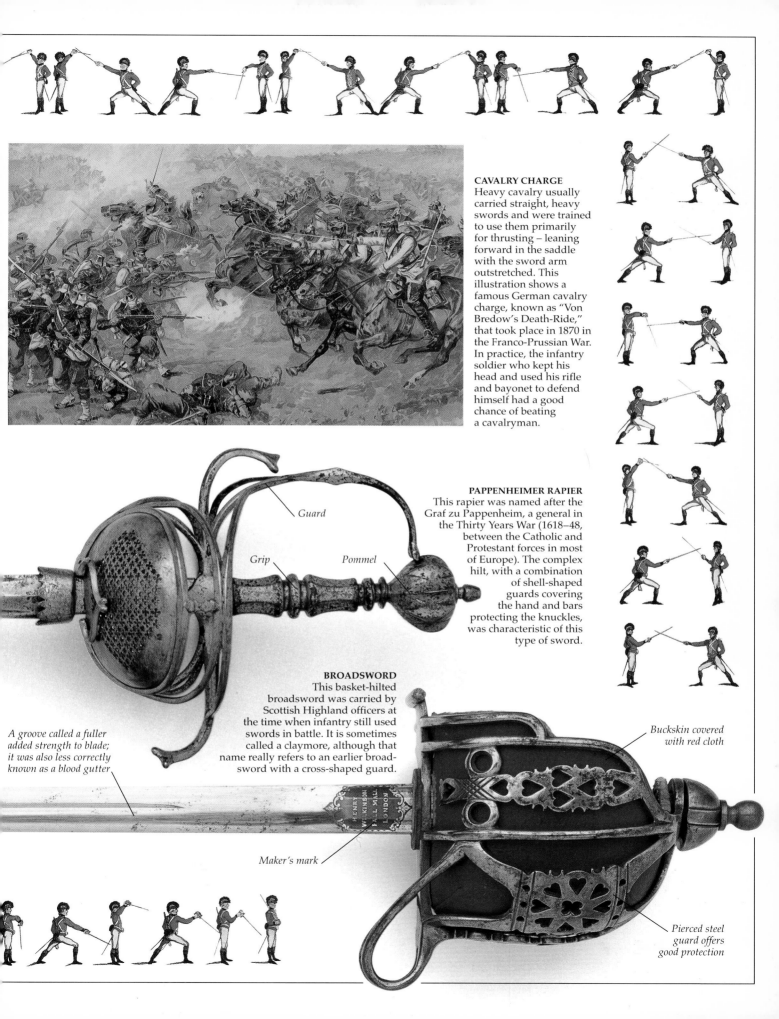

CAVALRY CHARGE
Heavy cavalry usually carried straight, heavy swords and were trained to use them primarily for thrusting – leaning forward in the saddle with the sword arm outstretched. This illustration shows a famous German cavalry charge, known as "Von Bredow's Death-Ride," that took place in 1870 in the Franco-Prussian War. In practice, the infantry soldier who kept his head and used his rifle and bayonet to defend himself had a good chance of beating a cavalryman.

PAPPENHEIMER RAPIER
This rapier was named after the Graf zu Pappenheim, a general in the Thirty Years War (1618–48, between the Catholic and Protestant forces in most of Europe). The complex hilt, with a combination of shell-shaped guards covering the hand and bars protecting the knuckles, was characteristic of this type of sword.

Guard

Grip

Pommel

BROADSWORD
This basket-hilted broadsword was carried by Scottish Highland officers at the time when infantry still used swords in battle. It is sometimes called a claymore, although that name really refers to an earlier broadsword with a cross-shaped guard.

A groove called a fuller added strength to blade; it was also less correctly known as a blood gutter

HENRY WILKINSON PALL MALL LONDON

Maker's mark

Buckskin covered with red cloth

Pierced steel guard offers good protection

Firearms

In THE 18TH AND 19TH centuries, most infantry soldiers carried a musket. It had a smoothbore barrel and was loaded by inserting powder and shot into the muzzle and ramming it home. It had a short range, and its black powder produced acrid smoke. A few specialists were equipped with rifles, whose barrels were cut with spiraling grooves that spun the bullet and improved its range and accuracy. Inventors had long experimented with breech-loading (rear-loading) weapons, but it was not until the middle of the 19th century that these became available on a large scale. Bayonets could be fitted to the weapon's muzzle for close-quarter fighting.

MUSKETEER
This Scottish musketeer carries a matchlock musket, ignited by a smoldering cord (the match).

Socket bayonet fitted into muzzle

Powder charges hang from bandolier

INFANTRY BATTLE
French and Prussian infantry in a bayonet fight at Hegelbord, 1813. Close-quarter combat like this was actually much rarer than many artists suggested, as the shock effect of approaching bayonets often persuaded enemy soldiers to run.

Cock holds flint

Frizzen struck by flint to produce spark

Barrel

Sling

Butt

THREE MUSKETEERS
On the left, a 17th-century French musketeer bites the end of his cartridge off before tipping the contents into his musket; in the center, a soldier rams home powder and shot, with the cartridge paper inserted last as wadding; on the right, a soldier "gives fire."

Lead shot

Patch box contains cloth patches, which were rammed down barrel to ensure snug fit of bullet

BULLET MOLD
This instrument was closed and filled with molten lead to make a musket ball.

Paper cartridge contained bullet and gunpowder

Lead musket balls

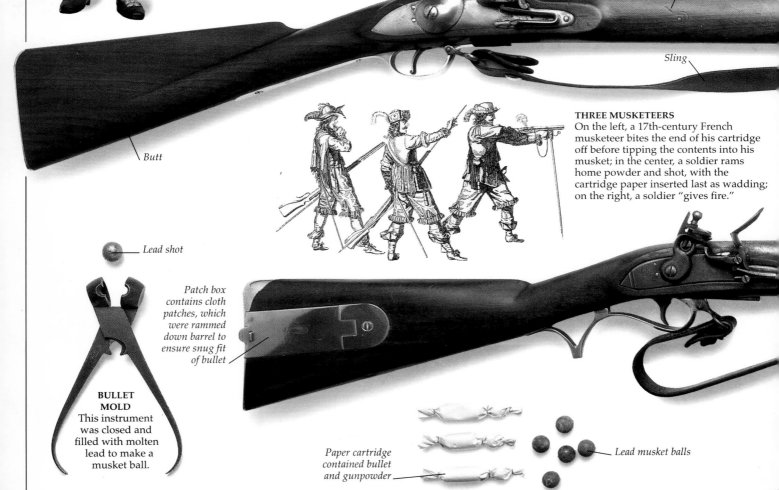

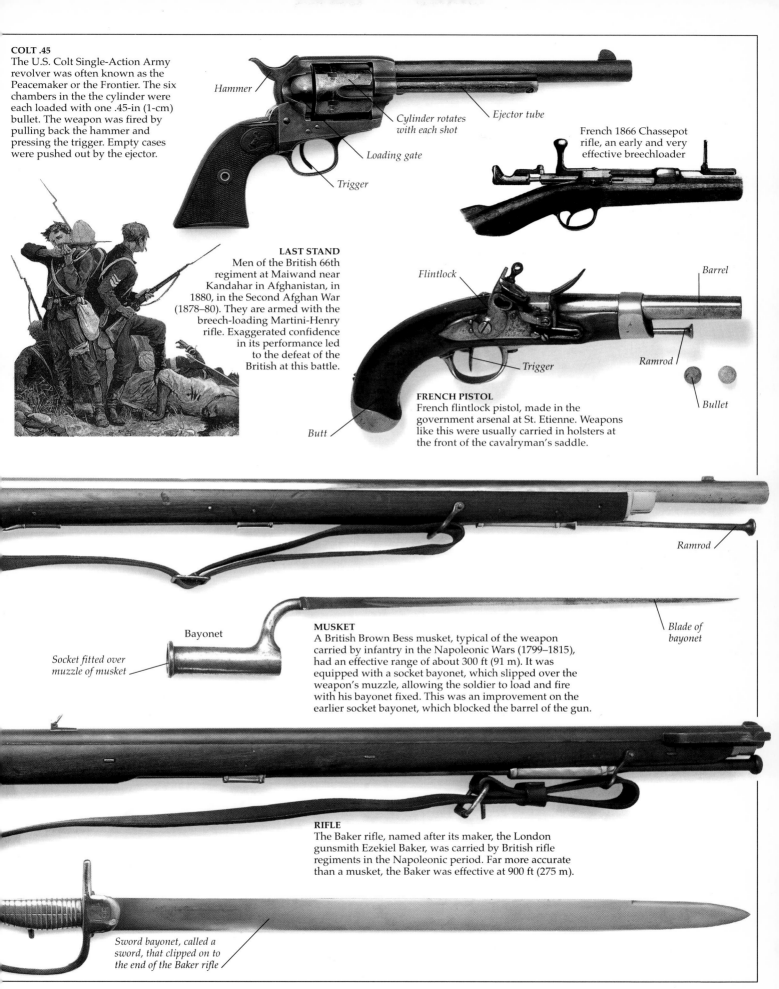

COLT .45
The U.S. Colt Single-Action Army revolver was often known as the Peacemaker or the Frontier. The six chambers in the the cylinder were each loaded with one .45-in (1-cm) bullet. The weapon was fired by pulling back the hammer and pressing the trigger. Empty cases were pushed out by the ejector.

Hammer

Cylinder rotates with each shot

Ejector tube

Loading gate

Trigger

French 1866 Chassepot rifle, an early and very effective breechloader

LAST STAND
Men of the British 66th regiment at Maiwand near Kandahar in Afghanistan, in 1880, in the Second Afghan War (1878–80). They are armed with the breech-loading Martini-Henry rifle. Exaggerated confidence in its performance led to the defeat of the British at this battle.

Flintlock

Barrel

Trigger

Ramrod

Bullet

Butt

FRENCH PISTOL
French flintlock pistol, made in the government arsenal at St. Etienne. Weapons like this were usually carried in holsters at the front of the cavalryman's saddle.

Ramrod

Bayonet

Socket fitted over muzzle of musket

Blade of bayonet

MUSKET
A British Brown Bess musket, typical of the weapon carried by infantry in the Napoleonic Wars (1799–1815), had an effective range of about 300 ft (91 m). It was equipped with a socket bayonet, which slipped over the weapon's muzzle, allowing the soldier to load and fire with his bayonet fixed. This was an improvement on the earlier socket bayonet, which blocked the barrel of the gun.

RIFLE
The Baker rifle, named after its maker, the London gunsmith Ezekiel Baker, was carried by British rifle regiments in the Napoleonic period. Far more accurate than a musket, the Baker was effective at 900 ft (275 m).

Sword bayonet, called a sword, that clipped on to the end of the Baker rifle

Close combat

STORM FROM THE EAST
Successive waves of invaders from Asia threatened Europe. These Mongol horsemen (p. 14), entirely at home in the saddle, were formidable opponents.

ANCIENT BATTLES were contests between warriors on foot or horseback. In close combat, they struck out with bronze or iron weapons, and used short-range missiles like arrows or javelins. Though battle tactics were usually simple, some commanders showed special skill, for example, by keeping a reserve of fresh troops at hand and using them when the enemy was exhausted. More often training or equipment gave the decisive advantage: the Roman army and the Greeks of Alexander the Great (356–323 B.C.) were well armed and well organized, and used carefully thought-out tactics. For thousands of years the infantry was superior, but with the invention of the stirrup, the cavalry reigned almost unchecked until the development of firearms.

Repair indicates that it was worn through many battles

Crest helped to deflect blows from enemy's sword

SAMURAI ARMOR
Samurai showed their status as a warrior class by wearing a pair of swords and elaborate armor made of plates of lacquered metal linked with colored silk cord. This gave them some protection from sword cuts in close combat.

WARRIOR QUEEN
Not all women stayed at home while their menfolk were hunters and warriors. In the first century A.D., Boudicca, the queen of a tribe living in East Anglia (England), fought against the occupying Romans. Although she destroyed three of the Romans' most important towns (London, St. Albans, and Colchester), she was eventually defeated by the Romans' superior tactics.

PRE-ETRUSCAN HELMET
Armor protected a soldier's most vulnerable points, and therefore added greatly to his chances of survival, but at the same time the weight slowed him down. This bronze helmet comes from Vulci in Italy and was made between 800 and 700 B.C. Although at this time iron had been introduced in Europe, bronze was still used for armor and weapons alike.

HALBERD DRILL
Weapons with a blade or a spike on a long wooden handle are called pole arms or staff weapons. A weapon of this type, the halberd, survived from medieval times to become the characteristic weapon of European infantry sergeants throughout the 18th century. These figures demonstrate halberd drill.

POLISH MACE
In the 17th century, Poland fielded formidable heavy cavalry who used lances, as well as maces like this early 17th-century specimen. The Polish king John Sobieski (1624–96) led the army that beat the Turks besieging Vienna in 1683, a victory that helped keep most of Europe out of Turkish control.

Swiss halberd, c. 1400

German poleax, early 16th century

Maker's mark

Sharp edge

REACHING OUT
Poleaxes and halberds increased the infantry soldiers' reach and were very useful if they were dealing with horsemen. The Swiss gained an awesome reputation by using pikemen, who carried long spears, assisted by halberdiers. Charles the Bold, duke of Burgundy (1433–77), was killed in battle against the Swiss at Nancy, his head split open by a halberd blow.

Langets (metal strips) protect staff

Mounted knights carry steel-tipped lances and a pennant

KNIGHT IN ARMOR
Armored knights, charging with lances on their heavy horses, were the dominant force in medieval Europe. There were some foes, like Swiss pikemen or English archers, whom they found hard to deal with. Monarchs liked to be depicted as knights even when these warriors were losing their value: this illustration shows the Emperor Charles V of Spain in 1529.

Gunpowder arms

THE INVENTION OF GUNPOWDER, a mixture of explosive chemicals, led to the invention of firearms. In these weapons a controlled explosion of gunpowder in one part of the firearm sent a bullet or a cannonball down a barrel. Gunpowder did not immediately transform war: in the 16th and 17th centuries a mixture of old and new techniques were used in battles, with swords and pikes alongside muskets and cannon. For most of that period, infantry and cavalry alike used firearms and edged weapons. Infantry consisted of pikemen, with body armor and long spears, and musketeers armed with muskets. Cavalrymen carried swords and pistols, but the steady increase of infantry firepower limited their effectiveness. Most armies drew up with their infantry in the center and the cavalry on the flanks. Cannon, still relatively cumbersome and primitive, were placed in the gaps between blocks of infantry.

FIRING A VOLLEY
"Ribaldequins" or "volley guns" had numerous barrels that were fired more or less simultaneously. In this specimen, shown in a French publication of 1630, the gunner fires the barrels one at a time.

OLIVER CROMWELL
Cromwell (1599–1658) was an English country gentleman and Member of Parliament who helped raise the Parliamentarian army on the outbreak of the English Civil War in 1642. He became lieutenant general (second-in-command) of the New Model Army and played a leading role in winning the decisive battle of Naseby (1645).

Cock (with flint) lowered onto revolving wheel

Revolving wheel with toothed edge

Trigger

PISTOLS
Muskets, with their longer barrels, were difficult to use on horseback. The first pistols, which were hand-held weapons, were wheel-lock pistols. The wheel was wound up with a key, and when the trigger was pressed it revolved, striking sparks from a flint held in the cock.

Ring for carrying cord

Rammer, to force charge and bullet down gun barrel

Nozzle

Wrench to wind up wheel on pistol

POWDER FLASK
The nozzle of this powder flask has two spring loaded catches. The one nearest the flask was opened to let powder flow into the nozzle. It was then closed, trapping a measured quantity of powder, which was loaded into the weapon by opening the upper catch.

GUSTAVUS ADOLPHUS
The Thirty Years War (1618–48), in which Protestants fought Catholics, was the most destructive conflict of the period in Europe. The Swedish king Gustavus Adolphus (1594–1632) was a champion of the Protestant cause. He produced a reliable professional army, which he commanded with skill and courage, only to be killed at Lützen, halfway through the conflict.

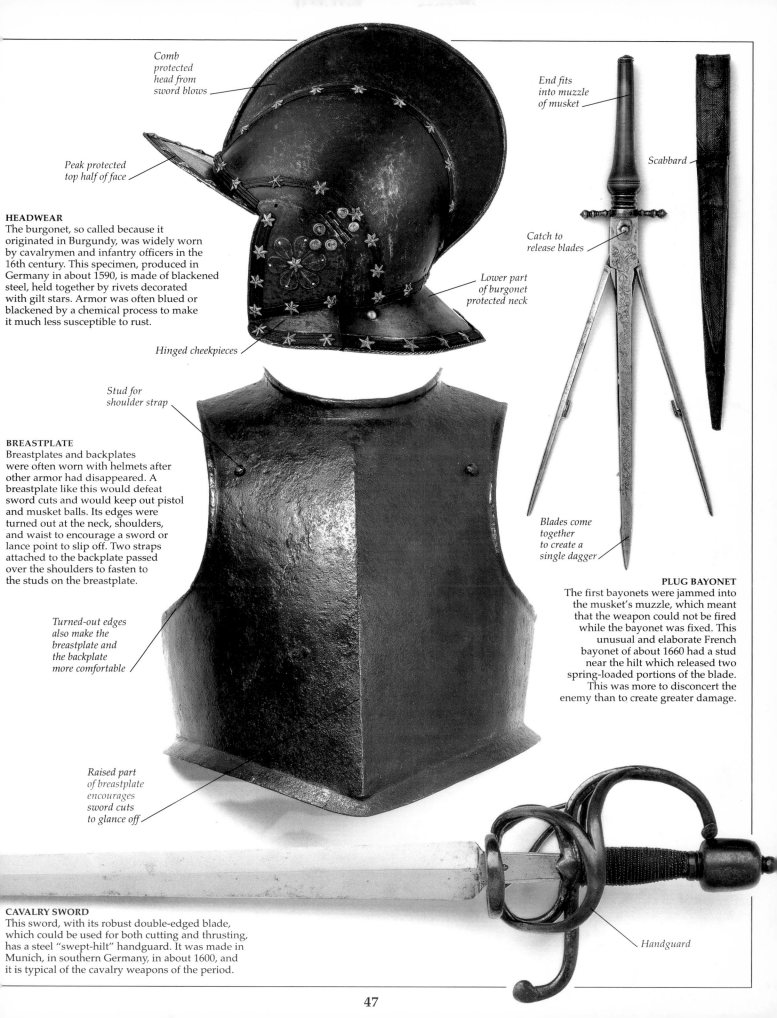

Comb
*protected
head from
sword blows*

Peak protected
top half of face

HEADWEAR
The burgonet, so called because it originated in Burgundy, was widely worn by cavalrymen and infantry officers in the 16th century. This specimen, produced in Germany in about 1590, is made of blackened steel, held together by rivets decorated with gilt stars. Armor was often blued or blackened by a chemical process to make it much less susceptible to rust.

Hinged cheekpieces

*Stud for
shoulder strap*

BREASTPLATE
Breastplates and backplates were often worn with helmets after other armor had disappeared. A breastplate like this would defeat sword cuts and would keep out pistol and musket balls. Its edges were turned out at the neck, shoulders, and waist to encourage a sword or lance point to slip off. Two straps attached to the backplate passed over the shoulders to fasten to the studs on the breastplate.

*Turned-out edges
also make the
breastplate and
the backplate
more comfortable*

*Raised part
of breastplate
encourages
sword cuts
to glance off*

*End fits
into muzzle
of musket*

Scabbard

*Catch to
release blades*

*Lower part
of burgonet
protected neck*

*Blades come
together
to create a
single dagger*

PLUG BAYONET
The first bayonets were jammed into the musket's muzzle, which meant that the weapon could not be fired while the bayonet was fixed. This unusual and elaborate French bayonet of about 1660 had a stud near the hilt which released two spring-loaded portions of the blade. This was more to disconcert the enemy than to create greater damage.

CAVALRY SWORD
This sword, with its robust double-edged blade, which could be used for both cutting and thrusting, has a steel "swept-hilt" handguard. It was made in Munich, in southern Germany, in about 1600, and it is typical of the cavalry weapons of the period.

Handguard

Large armies

In the early 18th century, battles took on a form they were to retain for many years. The majority of combatants were foot soldiers (infantry) armed with flintlock muskets, and battles centered on ferocious close-range exchanges of fire between the opposing infantrymen. Light cavalry scouted, screened (carried out counter-reconnaissance activities), and pursued, and heavy cavalry charged hostile horsemen and rode down shaken infantry. Cannonballs, multiple shot, and shells caused dreadful casualties in the enemy's close-packed ranks. For most of the 18th century, armies were composed of both volunteers and men recruited into service. King Frederick the Great (1713–86) tried to recruit foreigners so as not to ruin Prussian industry and agriculture: in 1768 he had 70,000 native soldiers in an army of 160,000. The French Revolution changed all this. In 1793 the revolutionary government, threatened by invasion, declared that all able-bodied men were to serve, and the army may have reached a million men in mid-1794, ushering in the age of mass armies.

Cartridge top held safely in place by button

AMMUNITION POUCH
This white metal pouch was made in the Caucasus in the late 18th century and would have contained paper cartridges for a musket or a pistol. There is a clip at the back for attaching it to the belt.

CARTRIDGE CASE
This cartridge case is one of a pair that buttoned onto its owner's coat. In the heat of action, it was important to have easy access to ammunition. Russian Cossacks wore these as late as World War II.

PISTOLS
Many cavalrymen carried a pair of pistols in holsters at the front of their saddles. These were made in the Caucasus, an area subject to Russian and Turkish influence, and are decorated with embossed silverwork that appears to have an Asian influence.

LIGHT DRAGOON
This private of the British 13th Light Dragoons is practicing parrying a cut aimed at his horse's head by an enemy horseman. His curved saber is typical of that carried by light cavalry, who used their swords for cutting rather than thrusting. His carbine (a short musket) would normally have been clipped to the carbine belt passing over his left shoulder. The 13th served with the Duke of Wellington in Spain in the Peninsular War (1808–14).

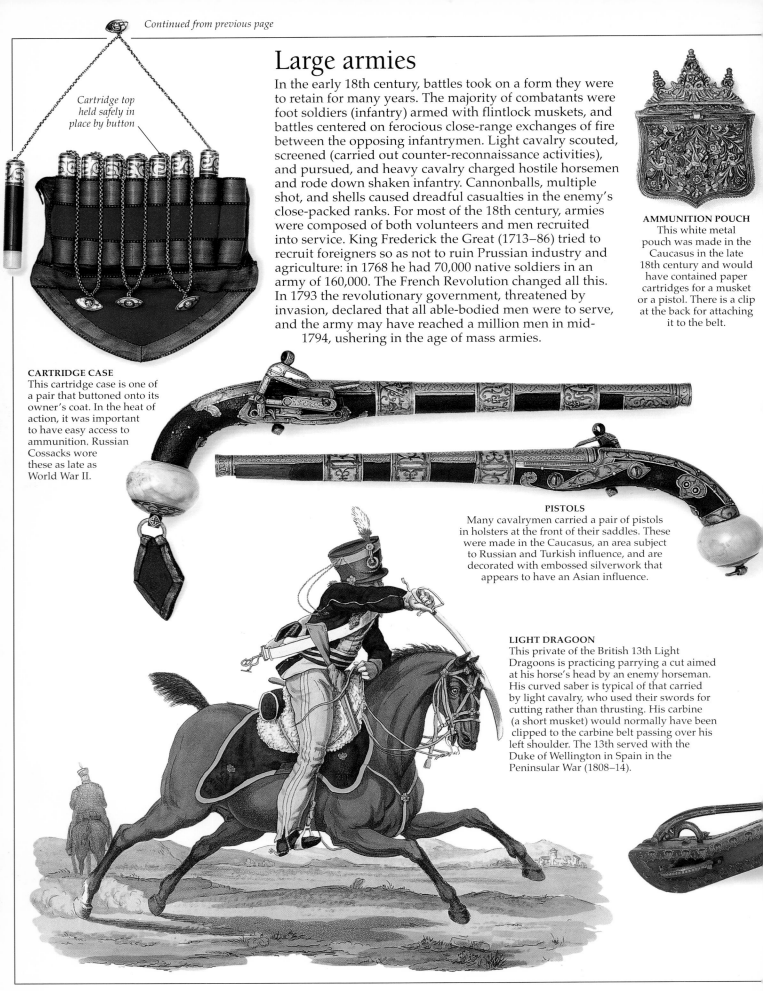

NAPOLEON

Napoleon Bonaparte (1769–1821) was an artillery officer who became emperor of the French in 1804. He dominated Europe, winning a series of victories, but exhausted his army when they retreated from Moscow in Russia's inhospitable winter (1812), and was then defeated at Waterloo (1815). He was brilliantly successful in using corps (large groups of regiments of all arms) that moved on separate routes but fought united.

DETTINGEN

In 1743 an Allied army under George II beat the French at Dettingen on the Main River. It was the last time a king of England commanded in battle. Contemporary illustrations fail to show just how smoky battlefields were. A veteran of an earlier battle saw no light "but what the fire of the volleys of shot gave."

6-lb (2.7-kg) cannonball

CANNONBALLS

Solid shot was the most common artillery projectile. Gunners usually tried to achieve a ricochet effect: they fired cannonballs that hit the ground just in front of their target and then bounced through it, causing casualties with every bound. This technique required firm ground, and the effect of Napoleon's main battery of guns at Waterloo was spoiled by soggy terrain.

Bronze gun barrel

Replacement gun carriage

BURMESE DRAGON

Superior military technology sometimes gave European armies a decisive advantage when they were fighting overseas, although determined local people who knew the land proved serious adversaries. Asian and African rulers sometimes hired European military experts and bought modern weapons. This cannon was made in Portugal for the king of Burma (now Myanmar). It is a decorative piece but would have worked had the need arisen. The barrel was captured by the British in 1885 and is mounted on a replacement carriage.

Rifled weapons

FROM THE MID-19TH CENTURY onward, technology changed the face of battle. Weapons gained accuracy when barrels were rifled (cut with spiraling grooves) and rate of fire increased with breech-loading (back-loading). Black powder was replaced by smokeless powder, and new high explosives enhanced the effect of shells. Machine guns developed into mobile weapons, which provided "the concentrated essence of infantry." It took armies some time to assimilate the effects of new technology, but the firepower revolution eventually produced battlefields that seemed strangely empty: by World War I (1914–18) armies took refuge in trenches. A British artillery officer wrote that "there were thousands of hidden men in front of me ... but nobody moved, everybody was waiting for the safety of darkness."

UNION TROOPS
Union soldiers at the battle of Antietam (1862). This battle of the Civil War between the Union army of the Potomac and the Confederate army of Northern Virginia caused over 22,000 casualties, the heaviest loss in U.S. history any day before or since.

BREECHLOADERS INTO BATTLE
The Franco-Prussian War of 1870–71 was the first war in which infantry-men on both sides carried breech-loaders. Heavy losses were suffered in charges against determined infantry. By the end of the war the Germans reduced casualties by attacking with "fire and maneuver" in which some soldiers fired while others rushed forward to fire in turn.

POM-POM AMMUNITION
By 1900 fast-firing light cannon were in service in several armies. Christened "pom-poms" because of their sound, they were subsequently used as anti-aircraft weapons.

Magazine gave out ammunition as it was needed

Foresight aligned with the backsight to aim gun

Backsight

Crank to fire gun

Gear to elevate (raise) and depress (lower) barrel

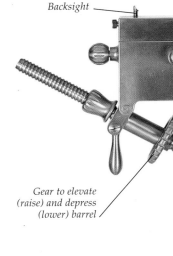

Tripod

GARDNER GUN
In 1874 William Gardner, who had served in the Civil War (1861–65), invented a machine gun that was much lighter than most contemporary weapons. Most of its versions had two barrels to create a high rate of fire, and some had five. The Gardner gun was adopted by the British Royal Navy, and unlike many early machine guns, it was actually used in battle, at El Teb and Tamai in the Sudan in 1884.

LEE-ENFIELD RIFLE

In 1902 the British army adopted the .303-in Lee-Enfield short magazine rifle as the best and latest technology. A trained soldier could fire at least 15 rounds a minute with it, and its effective range was up to 3,600 ft (1,097 m).

Sword bayonet

INDIAN WARS

In the 1870s, U.S. cavalrymen used single-shot Springfield carbines, but discovered that some of their opponents had traded hides for much superior Winchester repeaters.

U.S. cavalrymen in action during the Indian wars of the 1870s

BOER BANDOLIER

Ammunition consisting of smokeless powder in metallic cases was easy to carry and store.

RIFLED BARREL

Rifling describes the grooves in a weapon's barrel that spin the bullet to make it go farther faster. There were many systems. This is the Whitworth hexagonal system, used in some British-made cannon imported by the Confederates during the Civil War.

Twisted grooves

BATTLE OF FORT WAGNER

The Civil War was begun in part because of slavery. Slavery was banned in the North but economically important in the South. The Union army used black soldiers in segregated regiments with white officers. Five thousand Union soldiers, including the 54th Massachussetts Volunteers (all-black), attacked Fort Wagner in Charleston harbor on July 18, 1863. They reached the fort but could not take it, and lost 1,500 men.

ROBERT E. LEE

Lee (1807–70) commanded the main Confederate army during the Civil War. He defended northern Virginia, preventing superior Union armies from taking the Confederate capital of Richmond, and invaded the North twice.

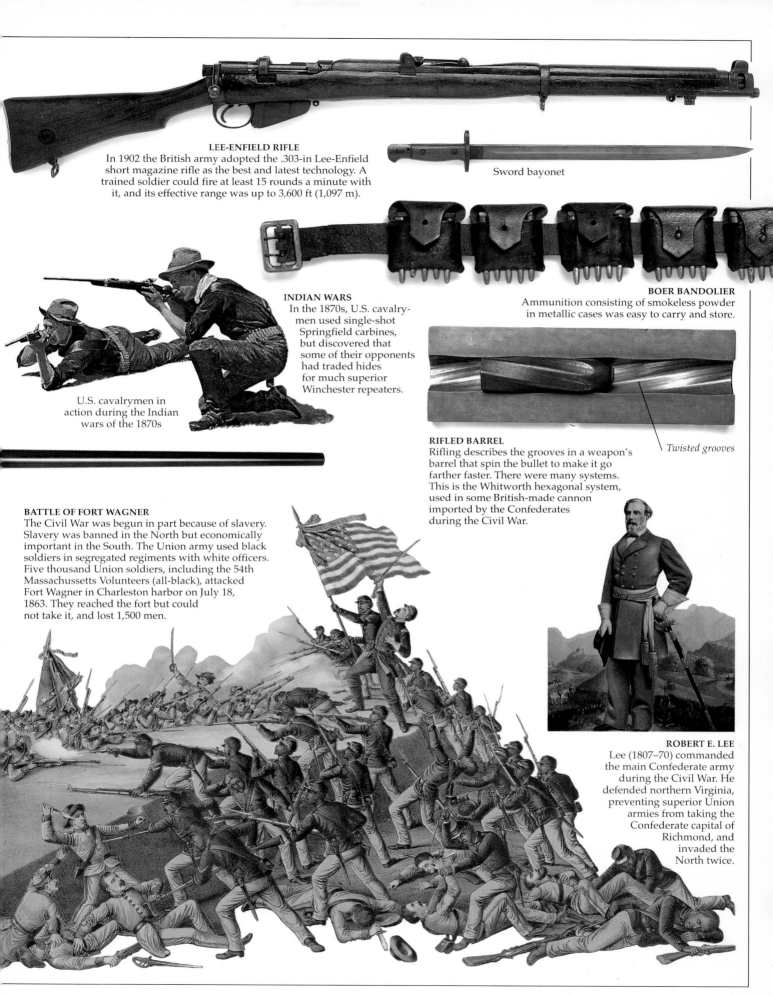

Communications

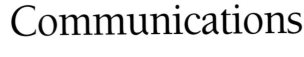

PIGEONS FOR RECONNAISSANCE
French cavalry in 1897 sending messages by carrier pigeons. The limitation was that the birds simply flew back to their lofts, so messages could only be sent one way.

UNITED STATES GENERAL Omar Bradley (1893–1981) wrote: "Congress makes a man a general; communications make him a commander." On the battlefield itself, soldiers needed to communicate, although their ability to do so was impeded by noise, smoke, and confusion. Senior commanders had to know what was happening in battle in order to commit fresh troops or change their line of attack. Often inadequate communications, not lack of skill or courage, ruined a promising plan. Until the development of the telegraph in the mid-19th century, communications changed little. Staff officers or messengers delivered verbal or written messages. Regimental officers used their own voices or relayed orders through drummers and trumpeters. Messages could be sent over longer distances by signaling systems or heliographs.

HELIOGRAPH
The heliograph, a tripod-mounted mirror, used sunlight to create flashes. Long and short flashes made up letters of the alphabet. It worked well in areas, like the Northwest Frontier of India, which were often sunny and had long views.

Sight

A heliograph's mirror could be adjusted to send messages in any direction

Tripod

MESSAGE HOLDERS
Pigeons with messages attached to their legs in holders like these were widely used during World War I (1914–18). The largely static nature of trench warfare reduced their limitations. The last message sent from Fort Vaux at Verdun, fiercely attacked by the Germans in 1916, asked for help and warned: "This is my last pigeon."

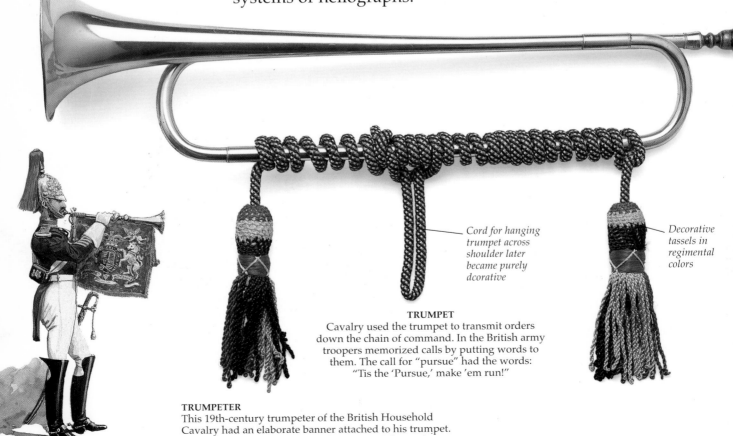

Cord for hanging trumpet across shoulder later became purely dcorative

Decorative tassels in regimental colors

TRUMPET
Cavalry used the trumpet to transmit orders down the chain of command. In the British army troopers memorized calls by putting words to them. The call for "pursue" had the words: "Tis the 'Pursue,' make 'em run!"

TRUMPETER
This 19th-century trumpeter of the British Household Cavalry had an elaborate banner attached to his trumpet. Banners were reserved mostly for ceremonial occasions.

SMOKE SIGNALS
The need for communication was not confined to formally organized armies. Native Americans were skilled at communicating by smoke signals, using a blanket to release smoke in puffs whose meaning could be understood by distant observers. One of the causes of Major General Custer's defeat by Sitting Bull at the battle at Little Big Horn (1876) was poor contact between advancing columns of cavalry.

WHISTLE
Whistle blasts could be distinguished in the din of battle, whereas shouts might not. Officers in rifle and light infantry regiments, whose men frequently were spread out, used whistles more often than their comrades in line regiments. The crossbelt, with an ammunition pouch at the back and a whistle suspended by a chain on the front, was widely worn by officers of rifle regiments and has been retained for full dress by the British Royal Green Jackets (p. 12).

DRUMMER
Drummers usually wore a uniform of their regiment's facing color (the color of the main uniform's collar and cuffs) with distinctive lace embellishments. This drummer belonged to the British 15th Light Dragoons in 1768.

Chain prevented whistle from being lost

Drum skin

Slider keeps drum skin taut

CIVIL WAR DRUM
Soldiers memorized tunes that regulated life in camp and transmitted orders on the battlefield. If an army was to form up ready to fight, its soldiers would be woken that morning by the long roll of the general call to arms, rather than by the usual reveille (the wake-up call). The drum was used by the infantry, although the bugle, with its better carrying power, became increasingly popular.

Wood shell

U.S. national symbol

The whistle was stored in this socket attached to the crossbelt when it was not in use

Engineering

MILITARY ENGINEERS helped an army to fight, move, and live. Engineers were particularly concerned with building permanent fortifications and with besieging fortresses. The French engineer Vauban (1633–1707) was responsible for a deep belt of fortifications protecting the borders of France. For many years engineer and artillery officers were better trained than infantry or cavalry officers, to reflect the need to master a range of technical skills. Engineers also constructed field fortifications (including trenches), built or destroyed bridges, made roads and, eventually, railroads, and improved the comfort and sanitation of barracks and camps. Some even established reputations as architects.

MEDIEVAL SIEGE
For centuries fortifications and siegecraft were the engineer's chief tasks. The walls of medieval castles were high and thick, and difficult to get over or through. Engineers for the attacking side often dug beneath them, making huge underground chambers with roofs held up by wooden props. These chambers, called mines, were packed with inflammable material. When it burned, the props collapsed, and with them the walls of the castle.

TRENCH LOOKOUT
In September 1914 the firepower of modern weapons helped freeze the war of mobility into the stalemate of trench warfare. Elaborate trench systems, with several mutually supporting lines, ran across Belgium and northern France.

Eyepiece

PERISCOPE
Trench warfare encouraged all sorts of ingenuity to enable soldiers to survive in what comfort could be found in trenches and dugouts. Because snipers (specially trained riflemen) were ready to shoot men who looked over the top of a trench, periscopes were produced, which enabled them to observe in safety.

TRAINING
Fortification was a science with rules that engineers had to master. These 19th-century British Royal Engineers trained by building a scale model of fortifications. The broad, low earth walls are designed to resist artillery fire.

Slope to absorb gun's recoil

BUILDING BRIDGES
Engineers built bridges as well as destroyed them. Some bridges rested on floating pontoons: others were suspended on ropes and poles.

Pedal to release cannon

EDELSBERG BRIDGE
A retreating army could buy time by destroying bridges, forcing the enemy to build their own. It was a matter of fine judgment as to when bridges should be demolished. Here we see the French attacking Austrians on a bridge near Vienna in 1809, while Austrian engineers try to hack it down to keep the French on the other side.

FRENCH SAPPER
Digging zig-zag trenches toward a besieged fortress was called "sapping," so engineers were often known as sappers. In most armies, infantry regiments contained specialists in field engineering. They were not as widely trained as proper engineers. These men carried axes and wore thick aprons to protect their uniforms. They often sported distinctive beards.

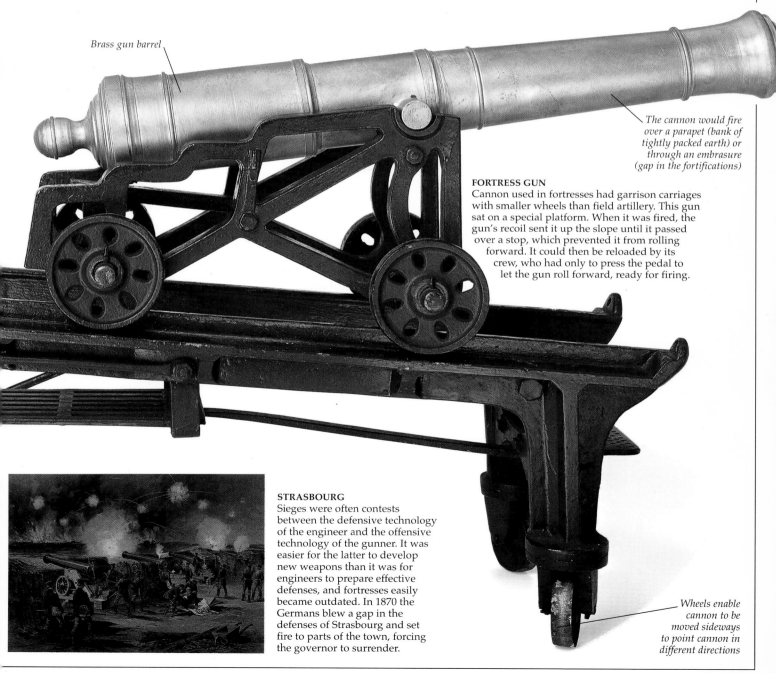

Brass gun barrel

The cannon would fire over a parapet (bank of tightly packed earth) or through an embrasure (gap in the fortifications)

FORTRESS GUN
Cannon used in fortresses had garrison carriages with smaller wheels than field artillery. This gun sat on a special platform. When it was fired, the gun's recoil sent it up the slope until it passed over a stop, which prevented it from rolling forward. It could then be reloaded by its crew, who had only to press the pedal to let the gun roll forward, ready for firing.

STRASBOURG
Sieges were often contests between the defensive technology of the engineer and the offensive technology of the gunner. It was easier for the latter to develop new weapons than it was for engineers to prepare effective defenses, and fortresses easily became outdated. In 1870 the Germans blew a gap in the defenses of Strasbourg and set fire to parts of the town, forcing the governor to surrender.

Wheels enable cannon to be moved sideways to point cannon in different directions

Victory and defeat

CORONATION OF NAPOLEON
In classical times the laurel symbolized victory, and successful Roman generals who were granted a "triumph" were crowned with laurel and rode through Rome in a chariot. Napoleon wore a crown of laurel at his coronation in 1804 to show that he was a victorious military leader.

ALTHOUGH SOME BATTLES ended in a draw, with no winner or loser, in most, one side defeated the other. Victory was indicated by the killing or capturing of large numbers of opponents, driving the enemy from the battlefield, or seizing a town or a geographical feature. Sometimes the effects of victory were far-reaching. The Battle of Waterloo (1815) ended the reign of Napoleon and led to a period of stability in Europe. But there was no guarantee that battle would be decisive, and sometimes a long war exhausted both sides. The victor's gains might not justify the human cost of battle. After Waterloo, the British commander, the Duke of Wellington, remarked: "I don't know what it is to lose a battle, but certainly nothing can be more painful than to gain one with the loss of so many of one's friends."

Big Elk, a warrior of the Omaha tribe

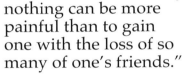
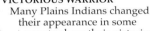

VICTORIOUS WARRIOR
Many Plains Indians changed their appearance in some way to show their victories. Big Elk, a warrior of the Omaha tribe, blackened his face to show that he had recently killed an enemy. Victory was also demonstrated by taunting an enemy with a non-lethal blow.

INSTRUMENTS OF VICTORY
Past victories can help win future ones. Soldiers were encouraged to take pride in their regiment's achievements, commemorated in battle honors emblazoned on its colors. These British guardsmen fought fiercely at the Battle of Inkerman (Crimea, 1855) although heavily outnumbered by attacking Russians. Their victory brought a new battle honor.

LOOTING AND PILLAGING
There was often a profit motive in war. Many European noblemen who went on the First Crusade in 1095 were landless younger sons hoping for land in the Middle East. Captured knights were held for ransom, and were released only when their families had paid the money. Common soldiers would pillage if allowed to: here we see a 14th-century army leaving a town it has just sacked, with livestock and other loot. Civilians were the real losers in most campaigns. They were robbed and maltreated by armies that passed by and a long conflict might leave little more than a desert behind it.

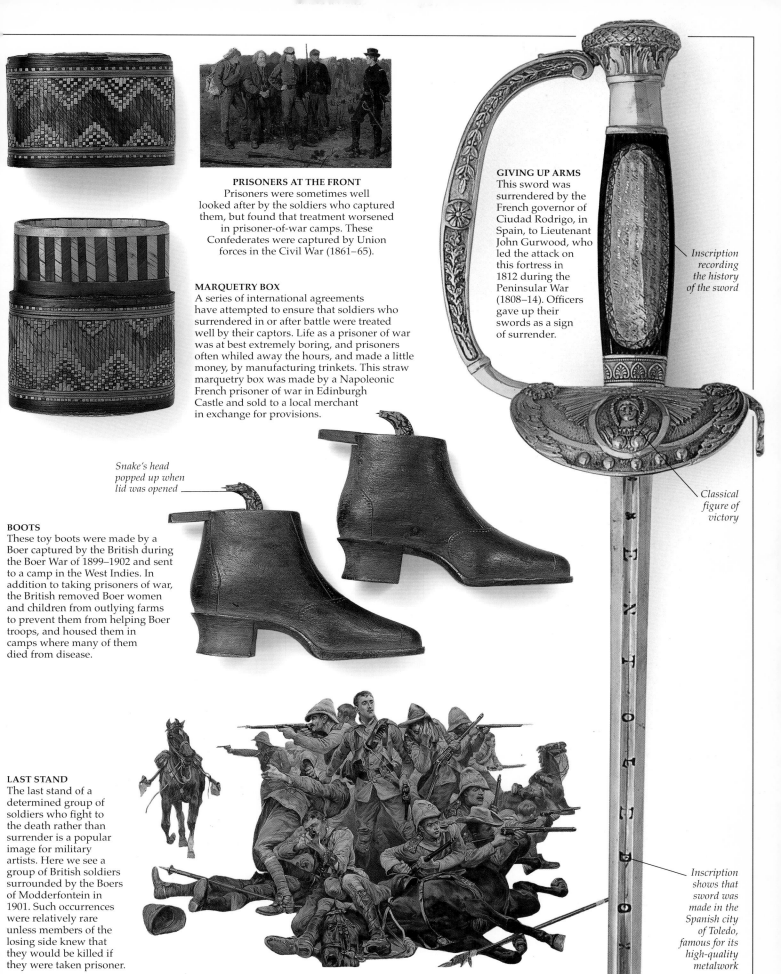

PRISONERS AT THE FRONT
Prisoners were sometimes well looked after by the soldiers who captured them, but found that treatment worsened in prisoner-of-war camps. These Confederates were captured by Union forces in the Civil War (1861–65).

MARQUETRY BOX
A series of international agreements have attempted to ensure that soldiers who surrendered in or after battle were treated well by their captors. Life as a prisoner of war was at best extremely boring, and prisoners often whiled away the hours, and made a little money, by manufacturing trinkets. This straw marquetry box was made by a Napoleonic French prisoner of war in Edinburgh Castle and sold to a local merchant in exchange for provisions.

GIVING UP ARMS
This sword was surrendered by the French governor of Ciudad Rodrigo, in Spain, to Lieutenant John Gurwood, who led the attack on this fortress in 1812 during the Peninsular War (1808–14). Officers gave up their swords as a sign of surrender.

Inscription recording the history of the sword

Classical figure of victory

Snake's head popped up when lid was opened

BOOTS
These toy boots were made by a Boer captured by the British during the Boer War of 1899–1902 and sent to a camp in the West Indies. In addition to taking prisoners of war, the British removed Boer women and children from outlying farms to prevent them from helping Boer troops, and housed them in camps where many of them died from disease.

Inscription shows that sword was made in the Spanish city of Toledo, famous for its high-quality metalwork

LAST STAND
The last stand of a determined group of soldiers who fight to the death rather than surrender is a popular image for military artists. Here we see a group of British soldiers surrounded by the Boers of Modderfontein in 1901. Such occurrences were relatively rare unless members of the losing side knew that they would be killed if they were taken prisoner.

Rewards of battle

REGIMENTAL ORDER
In Britain, medals were not generally issued until the 19th century, and this lack of official awards encouraged regiments to produce their own. This order of the 37th was instituted by Sir Eyre Coote of the 37th Regiment in 1774.

MEDALS, ORDERS, AND DECORATIONS are among the rewards of battle. Medals are given for gallantry; to commemorate an event; for service in a war, battle or campaign; and for long service or good conduct. Orders of knighthood hark back to medieval knights and have several classes – like a club with members of varying status. They are awarded for a variety of achievements, although some orders are specifically military. Decorations, which are granted for distinguished deeds or bravery, are generally superior to medals but usually lack the different classes found in orders.

DUKE OF WELLINGTON
The Duke of Wellington (1769–1852) commanded the British army that fought the French in Spain and at Waterloo. Here he wears his Gold Cross (a British decoration) as well as the stars of several orders, including the Spanish Order of the Golden Fleece. The Duke, like many senior officers in coalition armies, received numerous foreign orders.

ORDERS
Many orders of knighthood have separate military and civilian divisions, although some are purely military. In full dress uniform, knights wear the star of their order, and the more senior classes of knight wear, in addition, a broad sash over the shoulder. In undress (less formal) uniform, membership of an order will be shown simply by a ribbon worn on the left breast.

BRITAIN
The Most Honorable Order of the Bath traces its origins to 1399. This breast star was worn with a red sash.

FRANCE
The *Légion d'honneur* (Legion of Honor) was established by Napoleon in 1802. It had several classes, and could be awarded for military or civilian achievement.

THE NETHERLANDS
The Military Order of William was founded by King William I of the Netherlands in 1815, and was awarded for bravery, leadership, and devotion to duty in the presence of the enemy.

MEDALS FOR BRAVERY
Some awards can only be given for bravery in the face of the enemy and are open to servicemen of all ranks. They are often less elaborate than the badges or stars of orders, but are highly prized. A recipient of the Victoria Cross, for example, puts the letters VC, which follow his name, before those for any other awards.

The Victoria Cross, the most coveted British decoration, was instituted in 1856

The New Zealand Cross was instituted by the New Zealand government in 1869

The Medal of Honor, established in 1861, is the highest U.S. award for bravery

The German Iron Cross was freely awarded for acts of bravery

The Prussian order *Pour le Mérite* became the highest award for gallantry in action

The British Waterloo Medal was awarded to all ranks who were present at the battle (1815)

The Queen's South Africa medal was awarded to British soldiers who fought in the Boer War (1899–1902)

The bars on this Military General Service Medal mark actions in Spain in 1812

The Egyptian bronze star awarded to British soldiers in the Egyptian campaigns of 1882–85

CAMPAIGN MEDALS

Campaign medals are awarded to individuals for participation in particular campaigns. The different battles the soldier had fought in were named on bars attached to the ribbon; with some medals – for example, the Army Gold Medal – a new medal was awarded after a certain number of bars had been gained. The recipient's name is usually engraved around the rim of British campaign medals.

The Army Gold Medal was given to senior British officers who fought in specific battles in 1806–14

TURKEY

The Turkish Order of Osmanieh was first instituted in 1861–62 and was awarded to many British officers for their work in Egypt and the Sudan, which were then parts of the Turkish Empire.

RUSSIA

The Order of Saint Anne was founded in Germany in 1735, and was taken over as an Imperial Russian order in 1797. This is an early version of the insignia.

JAPAN

The star of the Japanese Order of the Rising Sun, which was established in 1875 and has eight classes.

PORTUGAL

The Portuguese Military Order of St. Benedict of Aviz began as a religious military order but became secular (non-religious) in 1789. Its badge (left) is a distinctive "cross fleury" enameled in green.

BRITAIN

The star of the Most Exalted Order of the Star of India, instituted by Queen Victoria in 1861.

Sick and wounded

A SURGEON AT WORK
This 16th-century German surgeon is removing a crossbow bolt from a soldier's chest. The French surgeon Ambroise Paré, who lived at this time, was one of the fathers of military medicine. He disagreed with treating wounds with boiling oil, and used a mixture of egg yolk, rose oil, and turpentine instead! With his English contemporaries, Paré did much to improve the status of military doctors.

WOUNDS AND DEATH are commonplace in war, but for hundreds of years many more soldiers died from disease than were killed by the enemy. Ignorance about the bacterial causes of disease meant that many simple wounds proved fatal, because they were not properly cleaned and because dirty instruments were used without being washed between operations. In the Civil War (1861–65), for example, 96,000 Union men died in battle, but almost twice as many died of disease. Discoveries in medicine and the organization of military medical services improved conditions, but it was not until the Boer War (1899–1902) that a soldier who had an amputation was more likely to survive than to die of gangrene.

RED CROSS ARMBAND
A Swiss banker called Henri Dunant was so shocked when he visited the battlefield of Solferino (Italy) in 1859 that he wrote a book about his experience. This led to the founding of the International Red Cross.

SURGEON'S SAW
At Waterloo (1815) the Earl of Uxbridge was hit just below the knee by one of the last cannon-shots fired. This saw was used to amputate his wounded limb. The Earl survived the operation and was fitted with an artificial limb. This earned him the nickname "Old Peg-Leg."

FLORENCE NIGHTINGALE
During the Crimean War (1853–56) the British base hospital at Scutari in Turkey was in an appalling state, with the sick and wounded lying in corridors, and toilets and drains overflowing. By November 1854 almost half the patients had died. That month Florence Nightingale (1820–1910) arrived with 38 nurses. Their efforts helped to reduce the death rate to just 2.3 percent within six months. There were others who worked to help wounded soldiers, such as Mary Seacole, a Jamaican nurse who also ran a shop.

NURSE'S INSTRUMENTS
Nurses needed instruments to help them dress patients' wounds, cut bandages, and take temperatures. During the Crimean War nursing became an integral part of the armed forces.

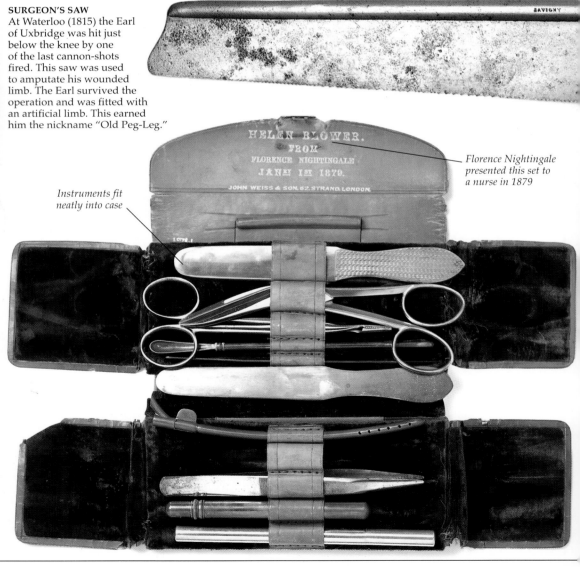

Florence Nightingale presented this set to a nurse in 1879

Instruments fit neatly into case

HELEN BLOWER.
FROM
FLORENCE NIGHTINGALE
JANY 1ST 1879.
JOHN WEISS & SON. 62. STRAND LONDON.

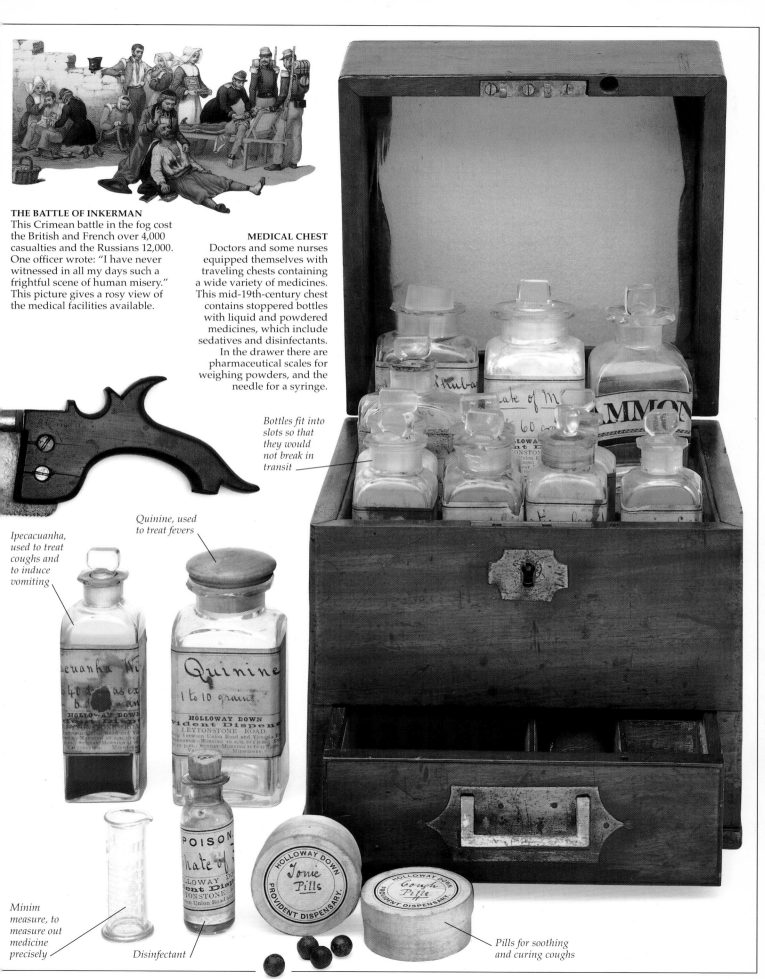

THE BATTLE OF INKERMAN
This Crimean battle in the fog cost the British and French over 4,000 casualties and the Russians 12,000. One officer wrote: "I have never witnessed in all my days such a frightful scene of human misery." This picture gives a rosy view of the medical facilities available.

MEDICAL CHEST
Doctors and some nurses equipped themselves with traveling chests containing a wide variety of medicines. This mid-19th-century chest contains stoppered bottles with liquid and powdered medicines, which include sedatives and disinfectants. In the drawer there are pharmaceutical scales for weighing powders, and the needle for a syringe.

Bottles fit into slots so that they would not break in transit

Ipecacuanha, used to treat coughs and to induce vomiting

Quinine, used to treat fevers

Minim measure, to measure out medicine precisely

Disinfectant

Pills for soothing and curing coughs

Memories of war

W<small>AR IS REMEMBERED</small> in many ways. Some participants thrust dark memories deep into their minds and prefer not to discuss their experiences. It is perhaps true to say that "those that know don't tell, and those that tell don't know." Others recall their exploits with pride, and look back to a time when they felt valued and had comrades upon whom they could rely. Societies often recognize the sacrifice that soldiers have made on their behalf, and commemorate their achievements with war memorials. All too often, though, returning soldiers found themselves neglected; when King Frederick the Great of Prussia (1712–86) saw ex-soldiers begging, he would sometimes say, "Drive the scum away." Other monarchs did their best for veterans. Louis XIV of France (1638–1715) established the Invalides in Paris as a home for wounded soldiers.

COMMEMORATIVE MEDAL
This British medal marks the 200th anniversary of the capture of Quebec by Major General James Wolfe in 1759.

Valley of the "Shadow of death"

FLOWERS OF THE FIELD
Even after casualties have been removed and nature has healed the scars, battlefields remain poignant places. Lady Hornby, the wife of the British commissioner to Turkey during the Crimean War (1853–56), pressed flowers from its battlefields. The flower (left) was picked in the "Valley of the Shadow of Death," the scene of the Charge of the Light Brigade (1854), and the flower (below) grew at Inkerman, the scene of another Crimean War battle that took place in 1854.

Inkermann

CAMERAMEN IN DANGER
Newspaper reports from battlefields provided an independent record of events, and helped civilians to understand the experience of combat. Newspapers were largely replaced by films and television.

MAN OF STONE

Edward the Black Prince (1330–76), eldest son of the British king Edward III, fought in the Hundred Years War (1337–1453) at Crécy and Poitiers, both in France. His nickname originated from his black armor. He was a successful soldier and was honored with a burial in Canterbury Cathedral beneath an effigy that shows him in full armor.

WAR MEMORIAL

Britain and its empire lost a million men in World War I (1914–18). Their memorials range from tablets in village churches to massive arches and obelisks. This one honors the British Foot Guards.

BURIAL

Prompt and reverent disposal of the dead is crucial for the morale of survivors: no soldier likes to think of lying forgotten on the battlefield. Here we see Japanese dead being buried during the Russo-Japanese War of 1904–5.

AMERICAN CEMETERY

It was not until World War I that burial of the dead was systematically organized. The policies then adopted by the British and Americans were continued into World War II. The American National Cemetery and Memorial at St.-Laurent in Normandy has 9,286 graves, including those of 34 pairs of brothers and one father and son.

CRUCIFIX

This crucifix was found on a dead Russian in the Crimea. The image of the crucified Christ is a compelling one for many Christian soldiers, who link their own suffering with his. Soldiers frequently became very attached to religious symbols and good-luck charms, and became deeply depressed if they were accidentally lost.

ICON

The unpredictable nature of war often deepens a soldier's religious faith (though sometimes it does the reverse) or makes him superstitious. Russian soldiers often carried icons (religious pictures) around their necks.

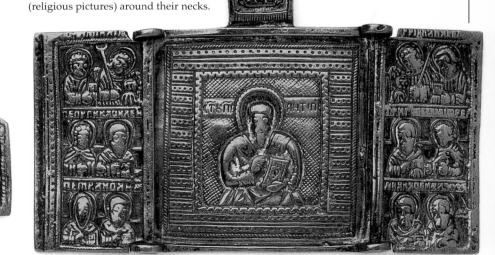

Index

Acknowledgments

Dorling Kindersley would like to thank:

For their help with photography and information:
95th Rifles and Re-enactment Living History Unit (Les Handscombe, Martin Handscombe, Dennis Wraight, Nick McMillan); the Army Museums Ogilby Trust; Angels and Bermans (film costumiers); the British Museum (Nick Nicholls of the photographic service); Mark Dennis; David Edge (Histrionix Ltd) and Mark Churms, Paul Ellis, Pierre-de-Hugo, Anthony Perkins, Chris Seidler, and Ian Smith; Freddie Edge; the Trustees of the Florence Nightingale Museum (and Timothy Bonham-Carter); Stephen Naegel; the Museum of Artillery in the Rotunda, (Stan Walter); the Royal Green Jackets Museum (Major R.D. Cassidy); the Trustees of the National Museums of Scotland (Scottish United Services Museum); the Sulgrave Manor Board, Northamptonshire; the Trustees of the Wallace Collection, London.

For additional special photography:
Peter Chadwick: pp. 30–31, 33, 49, 50.

For design and editorial help:
Mark Haygarth, Joseph Hoyle, Susan St. Louis, Gin von Noorden.

For the index: Hilary Bird.

Picture credits
(a = above, b = below, c = center, l = left, r = right, t = top)
Ancient Art and Architecture Collection: 14ar, 37ar, 56al;
Bridgeman Art Library / Bibliothèque Nationale, Paris: 36bl / British Library: 45br, 49al, 54ar / Imperial War Museum, London / (I Want you for the U.S. Army by James Montgomery Flagg, 1917): 8ar / John Spink Fine Watercolours, London: 9br / Private Collection: 38br;
Jean-Loup Charmet: 32al, 32cr, 32cl, 33bcr, 37bcl, 46ar / Bibliothèque des Arts Décoratifs: 33cr, 43ar;
e.t.archive: 16ar, 20cl, 21al, 24acl, 26bl, 36br, 44al, 52bl, 53al, 56br, 57bc / Bibliothèque Nationale, Paris: 7cl / Musée Malmaison: 49ar / Museum der Stadt Wien: 55al / Parker Gallery: 26br;
Mary Evans Picture Library: 12al, 13cr, 14cr, 15ar, 18br, 20bc, 25ar, 29cr, 31ar, 39acr, 41al, 42ar, 44cl, 46al, 50cl, 52ar, 54bc, 55bl, 60al, 60cl, 61al, 62bl, 63ar / Explorer Archives: 20al;
Fitzwilliam Museum, University of Cambridge: 16cr;
Robert Harding: 63cr / Musée de l'Armée: 55ar;
Michael Holford: 7ar, 15al;
Hulton-Deutsch Collection: 8al, 26bcr, 27bl, 28br, 30al, 34br, 34bl, 56ar;
Mansell Collection: 20cr, 36al, 36ar, 42bc;
Musée de l'Armée, Paris: 18al, 18-19a, 27br, 44ar;
© National Army Museum, London – photograph supplied by Bridgeman Art Library: 16br;
Peter Newark's Military Pictures: 10al, 19cr, 31br, 35al, 43al, 46bl, 51acl, 51bcr, 51bl, 53ac, 54acl, 56bl, 57tc, 58ar, 63tc;
Range / Bettmann: 50al;
Trustees of the Royal Hussars Museum: 25bcr;
Science Museum / Science & Society Picture Library: 25al;
Mr. A.D. Theobald, courtesy of the Royal Signals Museum: 52al.

Every effort has been made to trace the copyright holders of photographs, and we apologize for any unavoidable omissions.